ACCEPTED

God Heals A Broken Heart

D1259053

Nancy Z. Everist

First Printing, 2019

ISBN 978-1-7331058-0-4

Disclaimer: I have tried to recreate events, locales, and conversations from my memories of them. Some events have been compressed, and dialogue has been recreated from the author's journals and conversations with others involved in the original events. Because this is a book of memory, and memory has its own story to tell, I have done my best to make it tell a truthful account.

DEDICATION

To my beloved husband, Michael.
I value you as a man of integrity, honor and valor.
You have fought valiantly over me as protector and
walked with me as my best friend.
Abba has given me the most precious gift in you.
I am daily grateful for your life hid in Him.
Without your steadfast reliability, strength, and enduring
love shown to me in ways both big and small, this book
would never have been written.
Through your love, I know what it is to be cherished.

CONTENTS

INTRODUCTION

My story may not be yours.
My experiences may not be what you have lived.
No two stories are ever the same.

It is my prayerful hope that as you read through these
pages,you will come to see the unending love our Savior
demonstrates to each of us
in His diligent pursuit of our redemption.

This book tells of the journey we all must walk to find
peace and rest for our battle-weary hearts.
In that one small way, my story is everyone's story.

CHAPTER 1:

MOMMA COW

From my perch on top of the neatly stacked hay, I could hear the momma cow as she gently comforted her new arrival. I crept to the edge of the hay bales, quietly climbed down and slowly worked my way to the side rails of the calving pen.

Peeking between the wood slats, the momma cow and I briefly made eye contact. Not deemed a threat, she turned her attention back to her immediate task at hand. She gently nudged her calf, encouraging him to try out his spindly legs. He wasn't finding it easy to get all four of them working together. Just when he was able to stand, his momma's rough tongue that was working tirelessly to dry his wet ruffled hide would knock him off his unsteady hooves.

All the while, she used that special lowing sound that was reserved for the newborn. Its tenderness quieted the calf and bolstered his confidence to try again even though he was still dazed by his abrupt entry into this new world.

That soft lowing sound never failed to bring fresh tears to my eyes. They simply could not be held back as they quietly ran down my small round face. At the same time, I felt the familiar pain in my heart that caused my throat to burn and my chest to ache.

Living on a small farm in Oregon, I had seen this sight many times before. Regardless of how many, watching new life being warmly welcomed never ceased to reach the deep hidden places of my heart. It stirred a longing within me that had largely gone unfulfilled.

At 10 years old, I had learned early that the love available to me relied heavily on my performance. If I was a good girl, I was shown a cheap imitation of love. If I failed, then I was not desirable. In my world, failure meant bad things would happen. Life had already taught me this harsh reality.

Back in the farmhouse, there was an angry current that revealed its evil as a violent affair. Conflict raged. I had been driven to the barn this very day to escape the clash of wills, each desperate for the upper hand. In an odd sort of way, I saw these bouts as shallow attempts for some level of approval.

This time it was between my mom and older sister. Before I fled, I heard the slap, followed by the sound of a body hitting the kitchen wall. My sister's body. She was fiercely stubborn. If she was conscious, she would not quit. She was also strong and would fight back blow for blow. I could hear the screaming, yelling, and cursing as I retreated to my refuge in the barn. This day would not end well.

As I tried to block out the sights I had seen and the sounds that had chased me here, I was gripped by fear. It was seemingly my constant companion. Darkness shrouded my tender heart, and I was suffocating. It felt as if the weight of the world had settled on my small shoulders.

With every fiber of my being, I wanted the hurting to stop.

CHAPTER 2:

DID I KILL MY DADDY?

Not willing to walk into the aftermath of the battle back at the house, I climbed back up on the hay. I had lost count of the hours I spent out here.

As I lay in the quiet the barn offered, I couldn't help but think about my life and things that had transpired in my ten short years of living. My mind took me back to places and events I was struggling to understand.

Four years earlier, days before Christmas and my 7th birthday, my daddy died unexpectedly from a brain aneurysm. This reality was released in increments of information to me over several days. He was an organ donor, and recipients were being prepared while his body was sustained on life support. It was a long process.

For me, it began with my mom explaining my daddy was in the hospital and very sick. With the optimism of a child, I had full confidence that they would make him well, and he would be home soon. However, I had an inner sense my world was changing, and judging from the looks on the faces surrounding me, they were scary changes.

My mother, overwhelmed by this sudden change of circumstance, and left to manage four children alone, took me to a neighborhood babysitter. I spent my days waiting for my daddy to come home in that very dark place.

The very first day I got there, the man who lived in the babysitter's house touched me in places I didn't like. He would pull me down on top of him when he sat in his recliner. He used my body in ways that hurt. I didn't like him at all. He made me very afraid when we were left alone together.

I was terrified of him. This man was nothing like my daddy. When I did see my mother, I repeatedly asked if I could go see my daddy. Those requests always brought tears from my mom, followed by her refusal to take me to the hospital. I didn't like this place where I was being kept from the people I loved and desperately needed. I was scared and very alone. This was a bad place.

The touching by the man didn't stop. Quickly he became aggressive and bold in his actions towards me. Even as a child, I knew this was wrong. At first, I tried to fight him. Bad things happened when I did that.

I remember clearly the hurt, the chaos, and the emptiness I felt all around me. I could not grasp abuse. I wanted all of this to stop. I wanted to be home cuddled up safely in the arms of my daddy.

I had not been allowed to see my daddy in the hospital. The next news I received was that he had died and gone to heaven. My child's mind could not fathom death.
I was not allowed to attend the funeral. I stayed behind with the man who hurt me while they buried my daddy in the dirt.

I was left alone to wonder why my daddy wasn't coming back to get me.

When I was home, I would go into my fathers' bedroom and lay out his clothes on the bed. I would tuck the shirt into the pants, put the belt around them and fasten it, tuck his socks into the shoes at the end of the pant leg...and wait. I waited and waited for him to come back to me.

He never came. I couldn't understand why.

Shortly after the funeral, we visited my paternal grandmother. She wasn't warm and friendly, but rather scary. She and my mom argued a lot. Grandma had naturally taken her son's death very hard.

While at her house, I had gone upstairs to use the bathroom. She was very fussy about her house and followed me. I assumed she came to make sure I didn't make a mess. She didn't like messes at all.

When I was finished with my business, she made sure I washed my hands properly and used the correct towel to dry them. She then took me by the hand into a bedroom where she sat me down. She was very sad that my daddy had died and she was angry.

I didn't know why she was angry.

As we sat on the bed, she looked straight into my eyes. There she told me, "You know if you had been a good girl, your daddy would never have died. You always left your shoes in a mess, never putting them away straight. I kept my house clean so that nothing bad would happen. If only you had been a good girl, he never would have died. His dying was your fault."

Her accusations lodged firmly into the crevices of my seven-year-old brain. My child's heart absolutely broke in two.

I fled to my mother as those words chased me down the hall, down the stairs, and to the couch where she sat. When I got to her side, I was trembling and crying.
I am sure she thought I was just sad about things. My tears started her crying again, which made me more upset. I didn't have the courage to talk to her about it as my grandma glared at me from her chair.

I wanted to tell my mom how sorry I was. I wanted her to know I didn't mean to hurt my daddy, but I couldn't say anything.

There was seemingly no place of comfort for my aching heart. My grandmother's words were salt to the deep aching wound growing within.

I was stricken beyond words. My grandma said if I had been a good girl, he never would have died. The man said I was a bad girl and that's why my daddy wasn't coming back. I killed my daddy by not keeping my shoes straight and fighting the man.

At night, I had terrifying dreams and tormenting thoughts of my time with the man who had been given care over me while my daddy was dying. They left me feeling ashamed. I wondered what kind of horrible child I was to have such nasty thoughts. Children shouldn't think about such things; even I knew that.

CHAPTER 3:

THE NEIGHBOR

As I lay there, remembering, fresh tears filled my eyes. Ugly crying came from deep places in my soul. Even in my self-made haven, I had learned there wasn't any place to hide from the memories.

Even though night was falling quickly, nobody came looking for me. Nobody called me for dinner. So, I stayed on my perch where I felt the safest and continued thinking.

Just a few months previous, I had returned from spending a week with my maternal grandma and grandpa. It sounded like a great adventure at first. However, I felt a bit apprehensive when I watched my mom drive off.

My great-grandma was also staying at my grandparents' house. I had not known her much before this visit. She was old and stooped over, using a chair for support as she shuffled along. Unable to lift her head upright, she looked at you sideways. Since both my grandparents worked, she and I spent the days together.

Since moving was difficult for her, we spent most of our time sitting. She taught me how to do beadwork and tried to teach me to knit. We baked goodies together, her sitting and directing my every step. She enjoyed teaching me about the various flowers in the garden.

7

Every night before bed, she rubbed Vicks VapoRub on the soles of my feet before having me put on a clean pair of socks. That tenderness mixed with the smell of mentholatum made me feel warm clear to my insides. I would lean my head back on my pillow, close my eyes, and smile.

My great-grandmother was a woman of faith. She would read to me from the Daily Bread she had on her nightstand. Then she had me kneel down by the bed as I said newly-learned prayers. She would lovingly stroke my hair as she prayed, too.

I would crawl into the bed we shared, and she would sing hymns to me. Her favorite song was about a little brown Church in the Wildwood. I grew to love those special times we had together.

After being at my grandma's for a few days, I decided to take her little dog for a walk around the block while she was at work and great grandma was in her recliner. This is something I had done quite often on this visit. It made me feel so grown up.

I was a very friendly child because my heart was so starved to be loved. I enjoyed stopping to chat with the old neighbors as I walked along.

When I got to the home of one elderly man, he invited me inside for a piece of candy. I had visited him before with my grandma and knew he often gave gifts from his garden to his neighbors. He shared a common backyard with my grandma, and I could see her house through the window.

Once I got inside, I felt uneasy. He kept staring at me all over, and I didn't like it. I had seen the same look in his eyes from the man at the babysitter's a few years ago.

He came towards me with the candy dish held out. With each step closer to me that he took, my fear increased to the point that I couldn't move, and my stomach felt sick.

As I reached to take a piece, he grabbed my arm and pushed me down on the couch. He fell on top of me and began fondling my breasts. He reached for the zipper on my jeans, and I began to push him back.

Grandma's little dog began barking, sensing that I was in danger. I squirmed out from underneath this old man and ran out the front door with the little dog close on my heels.

I was panic-stricken! I could see him moving quickly to the backdoor. When he opened it, he began calling my name. I ran as fast as my little legs would carry me back to my grandma's house.

When I got there, I was sobbing and shaking. My great-grandma knew instantly that something was terribly wrong. I cried my story out to her. The first thing she did was pull me close next to her, trying to bring comfort. Then, she called the police. Her second call was to my grandmother at work.

My grandma arrived before the police. When she found out they had been called, she was very angry. She began yelling at my great-grandma, which upset me even further.

Why was she yelling?

As I listened to her words, I realized she was upset about what the neighbors were going to think with the police at her door. It was clear she didn't want the town folks to know about this. I felt ashamed for causing so much trouble.

When the police arrived, I was reluctant to share what had happened. My grandma was still angry, and it made me want to hold my tongue. My great-grandmother gently encouraged me to tell the whole story, start to finish.

Great-grandma sat, holding my hand with tears in her eyes. I could hear her praying under her breath. With her gentle coaxing, it gave me the courage to speak.

When I finished, my grandma was clearly embarrassed. She turned to the police and said, "Well, officer, this child has a history of lying. You can't trust anything she says. She has an overactive imagination. I doubt any of this really happened. I think it best if we just keep this quiet."

I looked at her, and I am sure my mouth dropped open. I could not believe what I was hearing.

The officer gently asked me if I was lying. I said quietly, "No. I am not lying." Again, my grandma insisted that I was a habitual liar and was doing this for attention.

Then, it hit me.

She didn't believe me! She thought I had made it up! I started to cry fresh tears. I told her I wanted to talk to my mother. I wanted to go home. My grandmother assured me she was calling my mom immediately, and she would have a long talk with her about my bad behavior. She wanted me to leave as much as I wanted to go.

The two police officers, one a woman, didn't seem very happy. They were reluctant to leave and kept glancing from one to the other. The woman officer was very kind to me and wanted to talk to me alone. My grandmother refused to allow it. The officers seemed frustrated. I thought they were mad at me so I wouldn't talk anymore. I simply couldn't find the courage.

Later, my great grandmother told me the officers were not mad at me at all. She said they were upset at my grandma's actions. Great-grandma tried to convince me the police believed me, but my heart had already shut down.

Years later, I found out that this elderly man had numerous complaints of child molestation against him. The officers had wanted me to talk to help stop this man but understood they needed the permission of my grandmother.

In this small community, nobody ever pressed charges because of the potential scandal. This man had been free to bring harm to innocent children until his death at over 80 years old. All this time, good people looked the other way.

My grandma was cold to me during the time I waited for my mother. She told me how very disappointed in me she was. She scolded me for wasting everyone's time, including the police. She made it clear to me she was going to have words with my mother when she came to get me.

Thankfully, my great-grandma did believe me. She sheltered me in her arms, singing and praying over me until my mother arrived days later to take me home.

True to her word, my grandmother and mother did have a long private conversation. I never knew what was spoken. I don't remember talking with my mother about what had happened as a child. Not on the long drive home, not until years later. I felt she was also ashamed of me, and I was embarrassed.

I longed for her to hold me close and tell me it wasn't my fault. There was a desperate need within me for her to listen and believe me. It was not to be.

I had no understanding of the darkness shrouding my heart. How could I have known my feet had stepped into an age-old trap seeking to steal the very life out of me?

Pure evil sat with its ugly arm around me, stroking my hair with its sharp bloody talons as it whispered thoughts into my mind. Consumed in my brokenness, I believed its lies.

My daddy died because I wasn't a good enough girl!

The babysitter man used me for his own perversion, and I was bad for fighting him!

An old man tried to molest me.

I was a liar!

All these things were my fault!

Big people said so. Big people knew stuff.

I was a child. They must be right.

I turned back to the scene before me. The cow gently nuzzled her calf.
As I listened to her lowing, it resounded within my love-starved heart.
How I yearned to be loved, comforted, and accepted with the same
tenderness I was watching between an old momma cow and her gangly
newborn.

I wondered for the umpteenth time: would anyone ever love me with
the same love I heard in that sound?

With all my heart, I wanted to be loved more than my next breath.

Could it ever be?

CHAPTER 4:

WHY DON'T YOU HATE GOD?

I've had sweet opportunities to share this part of my story with people whose lives have been shattered by various pain. One of the most frequent questions I've received is, "How, after everything you went through, could you ever love a God who did that to you?"

These words hurt me deeply, but I understand the source of the question. When I heard that, I felt I'd not done a thorough job in sharing my story and my beloved Heavenly Father was being blamed for the pain in my life. There is no greater grief to me than to see that happen.

I could never blame God for failing me because He was the One who carried me through the darkness.

It was His arms that wrapped around me and held me close in those early days of pain and heartache and the ones yet to come. It was His Voice that whispered words of peace and comfort into the depths of my being. His strength sustained me when my tiny heart grew faint. Hope found only in Him drove out the despair wanting to suck me beneath the dark waters of sin and death forever.

Even as I speak now of how present He was with me through each dark valley, people who've known their own pain rise up and say, "But He could have stopped it, and He didn't!"

13

At this point, they are no longer talking about me or my story. They are fully living their own painful memories played out in living color before their eyes. They are crying out from their own agony of heart, maybe for the first time ever. There's nothing to do but hold them close and let the tears flow until there aren't any more to cry.

I'm not special or unique, and I don't cover the pain. I simply understand that God wasn't doing me harm. Quite the contrary. He was helping me survive. Even more than that, my pain mattered to Him.

One of the greatest tragedies a human heart can suffer does not come from the hand of men. I know something of the cruelty of evil men, and it seems bottomless. With that said, the great tragedy comes when a heart has been broken, and those who have suffered harm turn and blame God for the evil they have endured.

If that happens, two things happen simultaneously.

First, immediately, the darkness wins. It has succeeded in maligning the character of our loving Father and driving a wedge between Him and us. Once we separate ourselves from Him, all hope is lost.

Secondly, we are filled with bitterness that keeps us from receiving the healing we so desperately need. Bitterness corrodes us from the inside out and causes more damage than anything we could suffer at the hands of people.

Far too many people live and die in that horrible tormenting state of bitterness. Their pain becomes the barrier keeping them from finding their way into freedom. Sadly, it is of these precious people it is often said, people who have been hurt will hurt people. It is a heartbreaking thing to behold.

Be encouraged. It doesn't have to be that way. I was caught in that trap for a number of years, and there is freedom from this dark place.

The Truth that needs to be understood, in the midst of any kind of abuse and suffering we may endure, is that we are all created with a free will. We love to talk of our freedom to make our own choices and pride ourselves in this freedom. When it is used well, with good intentions towards others, it is a beautiful gift, a priceless commodity.

However, there are those who choose to use their free will to bring great harm. That harm can be big or small, but harm is harm. Those who walk in evil are just as free to choose how they will engage with others. We have laws that govern what is acceptable behavior, and the consequences when those laws are violated.

However, laws do not change the heart of man. Laws are powerless to transform a man's character towards goodness when he has set his will on destruction.

So, let's take a deeper look at this and really think it through.

If God were to stop those people from doing harm by removing their freedom to choose to follow evil, He would also need to take away our freedom to choose to do good and be His light in the darkness. It can't be one-sided. It must apply equally to all.

Another crucial point to understand is to develop an eternal mindset. We all know this life is fleeting. There's so much more coming that is far beyond our comprehension. Nobody gets away with evil behavior regardless of how things appear.

You may not see the vengeance your pain demands, but we have a just and faithful Father who is Judge over all. Every one of our words and deeds is being recorded in heaven. We all will give account for our choices – good or bad.

In all my years, I didn't blame God for the evil that came my way. In my life, that would have meant He was the cause of the evil. This is not how I knew Him and not how He revealed Himself to me. He was everything good in my life; at times, the only good thing. He defended and protected me numerous times.

In the midst of great darkness, He never let me go. He heard the cry of my tender heart, and He came.

Truth be told, He raised me.

Back to my story.

There's so much more I need to share.

CHAPTER 5:

MY FATHER'S ARMS

Could it ever be? The words no sooner left my mouth that day on the hay when I felt those familiar arms wrap around me. My heart calmed, and the tears slowed as a sweet peace began to envelop me.

This wasn't the first time, and I hoped with everything within me that it wouldn't be the last. I didn't understand it, but it didn't seem to be the kind of thing you were supposed to understand. It just was.

That was enough for my child's heart. It just was!

Within a few months after my daddy passed away, my mother re-married. At first, I was ecstatic at the idea of having a daddy again. It didn't take too long to realize that this man wasn't like my daddy. He wanted to be left alone when he came home from work. I was not allowed to talk about my old daddy. He drank, my mom and he fought, and our home was filled with anger.

Blending two families is not an easy task. Ours was not going well on any front. The move from Portland to this small rural farm was an attempt to bring some semblance of newness. It wasn't working for the family - not by any means.

It was, however, working for me! I absolutely loved being outdoors. It became my playground, and I explored every inch of it as much as I could.

17

Chores? No problem! I was eager to be outside and away from the house. I spent hours walking the fields, following the fence lines that ran below our place, discovering wildflowers and picking blackberries. I loved being out chopping wood, moving hay, and cleaning stalls.

I would often go down to the creek that flowed below our place and sit on a rock. I would close my eyes, and I could feel those arms wrap around me. As my heart was quieted, I could hear music in the sound of the water running over the rocks. It felt like angels were singing over me. I didn't understand the words, but I knew peace was filling those empty places within me.

Looking back on it now, I have to wonder why no one came looking for me. I would often head off on foot or on my horse with no particular destination in mind - anything to be away from the house.

I got lost more than a time or two, and an old farmer whose barn I came across would load up my horse and me and bring us home. Or, I would leave my horse in their barn, and they would drive me home until I could swing back by and ride her home in the daylight. The only response was anger at me for bothering the neighbors.

As I walked or rode, I would talk to God. Nobody had told me the arms I felt around me were God's, but I seemed to know it deep within me.

One time I was riding through a neighbor's orchard when my horse spooked and took off. She took me right under a low branch that knocked me off backwards. I fell hard, and my back landed on a rock. I felt a shock like an electric jolt go through me and then nothing. All I could do was lay there. Nobody knew where I was, and I started to get scared.

Then those arms wrapped around me. Peace came, and I could feel a warmth spread through my body. It was like liquid strength was being poured into me from the top of my head to the tips of my toes. Then I heard comforting words telling me all was well and encouraging me to sit up. My horse hadn't moved an inch and was still standing next to me. I sat up, then stood and felt fine. I mounted, and we continued our ride home.

All the way back to the barn, I kept thinking about what happened.

So many stories like these happened over and over in my life. These brushes created a hunger to know this God, who always seemed to be with me, and especially in times when I was in trouble.

Who was He?

How did I get to know Him?

For my 12th birthday, I didn't ask for anything other than a Bible. I don't know if my folks thought that was an odd request or not but since it was all I asked for, I got it.

I felt like the richest person in the world! I read this precious book cover to cover, again and again. I jumped and skipped through it and became familiar with its pages. I learned more and more about God. I read the things Jesus did when He was alive. I loved the apostles' teaching because, through them, my moral compass was being developed. I saw in its rich pages the life I wanted to live. My Bible was very precious to me.

Being a child, I simply believed what I read. I didn't question it; I absorbed it. It was being grafted into the core of my being.

At this same time, my older sister was studying to be a witch. Oregon has been declared and claimed as sacred land by Satanists, and witchcraft is prevalent. She was very involved with drama at her high school, and somehow her interest in witchcraft was sparked. The two very different paths under the same roof created an evil dynamic in an already anger-infused environment.

She and I were at constant odds, and she hated me. Truly, hated me.

Since my folks were basically newlyweds, they would often go away for the weekend. Those were hellish times in my life. That left my sister or older stepbrother in charge. That meant horror for me.

My older siblings enjoyed terrorizing me. My stepbrother delighted to invoke fear in cruel ways. My sister would feed her craft through demonically-infused movies, and demons would come. I had read about demons in the Bible and angels also. I knew there was a great battle between them, and it raged all around our home. And yes, I saw them.

I also read in my Bible how demons had to leave when Jesus said so! I didn't have a deep understanding of how it worked, but I had childlike faith to believe it would.

I would ask Jesus to make those demons go away when they tried to pounce on me or come to hurt me. He answered the cry of my heart, and they left. This made my sister very angry because her spells and incantations weren't working.

It made me feel safe.

I would run to my bed, pull the covers over my head and sing the songs to Him I had heard the angels sing. They were made up songs because I didn't know them, but they flowed from my heart. Somehow, I could feel God was happy with the songs.

As I read my Bible, I was learning and gaining some understanding. It seemed to ooze into the crevices of my heart and it brought comfort to me.

Even still, the battle around me continued to rage.

CHAPTER 6:

UGLY LOVE

My teenage heart craved affirmation from my stepdad that a little girl's heart desires. Sadly, that never came. I made him happy or at least satisfied mostly by not causing trouble and staying out of his way.

I wondered, as most young girls do, if I was pretty. I would stand in front of the mirror dressed in the best I had to wear. I would turn this way and that, trying to see myself as others did.

Was I pretty? Was I desirable?

On one such occasion, my stepdad saw me through the open crack in my door. We made eye contact, and I was embarrassed at being caught striking a pose in front of the mirror. I was developing my girlish curves, and uncomfortable in this new body that seemed to have taken over without my permission.

Standing before the mirror, feeling very exposed and vulnerable, he stepped in, looked at me and smirked. "Don't get your hopes up. Your shoulder blades stick out farther than your boobs." He walked out, leaving me humiliated.

My mom and stepdad were very cutting with their words. They would tease in a cruel fashion. My stepdad would tease me about being fat and nicknamed me "Fatima."

My mother would tease and say that I never had to worry about anyone stealing me. "Once they got you under the first street light and saw what you looked like, they won't be able to get you back fast enough!"

They would say I was a twin, and the pretty one died.

In this house, you were expected to laugh with a brave smile. If not, you were mocked for not having a good sense of humor and considered weak. You never dared showed weakness in my home.

I learned at an early age that cruelty, when delivered with joking, goes deep. Not only are the words cutting, but you feel foolish for being sensitive to them. After all, they were only kidding, right?

Their words hurt deeply, but I felt powerless to stop them.

Little girls crave approval from their parents, and especially their daddies. I was no different.

Their words kept the wounds raw and bleeding, making me vulnerable to more wounding. Each cruel remark was one more stone in the wall that was being built around my heart. It was a wall for self-protection. Since there was no place to hide, it was the only way I knew to keep out the pain.

The words reinforced the torment that had taken my heart captive. If my parents couldn't love me and saw no value in me, I must be unlovable and valueless.

Something in me broke a bit more, but I quickly resigned myself to accept this as fact. To fill the gap, I became driven to prove my value.

My four older siblings created a great deal of heartache for my folks. It was difficult to outlive the reputation they left in our small country town and the county in which we lived.

Due to their drug, sex, and alcohol abuse, our family name did not carry warm fuzzy feelings when spoken in the community. Definitely not with the local authorities.

I watched my parents being called down to the police station more than once. I saw their grief over the choices their children were making. In spite of the fact I didn't feel close to them, it bothered me to see them hurting. I didn't want to bring my folks any more shame.

Feeling responsible, I decided to work hard at setting a better example for my only baby sister to follow. I wanted to change our family's reputation and make my parents proud.

Outwardly, people admired my zeal, appreciated my drive, acknowledged my academics, and seemed to forever comment on my strength. Inwardly, my drive to earn love, approval, and be accepted had been grossly misinterpreted by the adults around me as maturity.

Like an addict, the high I got from the temporary applause was not satisfying my need to be loved. I was always looking for new ways to excel, new ways to fill the void. I needed more and more as the emptiness grew.

I had not experienced any meaningful relationships in my life. I had no understanding of commitment or what a healthy relationship looked like.

The "love" I saw between my mother and stepdad was a punch on the arm so hard it brought tears to my mother's eyes. It was cruel words, cutting sarcasm and no tenderness. It was yelling, screaming, cursing, and slammed doors, with raised voices on the other side and violence.

My experience with men was limited to being forcefully subdued for their own perverse pleasure. I was an object to be used with no respect or concern for basic human decency.

I thought this was how relationships were between men and women.

I was very broken in this area. Worse, I had wholeheartedly accepted the condemnation deep within that I would never find love. There was no resistance in me to the judgments being levied against my value as a person. I saw nothing else to prove those accusations wrong.

Up to this point in my life, I had avoided dating, having no interest in being married, or having a family. I was working hard to excel in academics. I wanted to be a social worker or a doctor. I was 17, a junior in high school slated to graduate early. It appeared I had high goals, but I was so lost. There was little to no direction or encouragement from the adults in my life, other than to get out of the house by 18.

My older sister had several young men calling on her. She was beautiful and very talented. I admired her secretly, even though I was terrified of her.

I watched these boys come and go in her life. She delighted in playing with their hearts and moving on to the next one. When one particular young man came calling, only to have her reject him, he turned his attention to me.

I was very immature, naïve, and unprepared for the flattery of being noticed. I wasn't attracted to him as a person. I was attracted to the feeling of being seen.

With a heart longing to be loved, it should be no surprise my first experience with dating quickly fell into sexual sin. This act was a dire consequence of too much buried pain and too little guidance. He was not an evil person, and I don't believe he set out to hurt me. The problem was, I didn't know what it meant to be loved or how to love. In his way, I imagine he loved me as he said he did.

Be that as it may, this was a very bad turning point in my life. That fall felt like a jump off Niagara Falls, leaving me even more devastated. I didn't even know that was possible until I found myself falling headlong into despair.

If there had been any doubt in my mind, it was now utterly removed. I now knew exactly what I was. Dirty, damaged, used, and undesirable as a person, only as an object. I saw myself completely beyond repair.

My next thought was even more horrifying. I knew from reading my Bible; this wasn't okay with God. This broke the moral code I had set for myself. With this realization, it nearly came to be the end of me.

Are there words to explain what happens to a heart when it has utterly betrayed its only hope? If there are, I've not been able to find them.

Anything I attempt to say would never describe the guilt and shame that took up residence within me that day.

I had failed the One I loved the most.

Now, He was going to abandon me, too.

The worst part was, I deserved it.

Not knowing what else to do, I ran from Him.

Nancy Z. Everist

CHAPTER 7:

RUNNING

The next few years of my life were some of the loneliest I've lived. I couldn't face God and what I had done. I felt as if my life was over, and I needed a ticket out of town.

This young man must have sensed the guilt that buried me. I'm sure in his way, he felt a sense of responsibility for me. In short order, we were married. I knew it was a mistake, but there was no strength of character to admit it to myself.

One of the most cynical sides of brokenness is how it affects the people in our lives. Regardless of the motives good people may come into your life with, the tentacles of pain reach out to them.

I caused this man undue harm because of my own wounding. He didn't deserve it. Nobody deserves to be treated wrongly.

I was too immature to see any of that then. It would take me years to heal enough to acknowledge it.

Pain has no boundaries and is far-reaching in the destruction it brings.

Out of the dark place that filled my life, I daily grew to resent him. He tried, and that speaks to his character. I simply was not in a place to receive any semblance of love, no matter what the intention was. He was not perfect, but I would be remiss in laying anything to his charge.

Again, each one of us will give an account for our actions, and my responsibility lies with me owning my part.

Within the first three months, I got pregnant. If there was a hopeful time in this short marriage, that was it. In the midst of the agonies of my heart, I had a new purpose and meaning. I instantly fell in love with my unborn child.

At 18, I was a mommy. Is there anything more overwhelming as having a small bundle of life placed in your arms knowing you are responsible for their wellbeing?

The first time the nurse brought my baby to me, I begged her not to leave us alone. She smiled at me with understanding and stayed. Together we undressed her, counted fingers and toes, gazed at her beauty and talked baby stuff. I was so grateful for this nurse's kindness to a young and scared new momma.

That I loved this precious little one with all my heart, there was no doubt! I'm not sure where it came from, but it welled up in me like a spring. I was so humbled by her.

And I was terrified.

I couldn't help wondering what I had to offer this little one.

Through the following year, this child became my life. I poured the best of all I had into her. She brought me such happiness. She was my reason to greet each new day. I would rock her well into the night, long after she was asleep, just to feel her in my arms.

The unconditional love a child gives helped to ease the ache in my heart. For a time, she filled the void that had been empty in my life.

As babies do, she started growing up and becoming a bit more independent with each developmental milestone. As she spread her wings, the emptiness in my life began to haunt me when the house would grow quiet.

The less she needed me, the more I was forced to deal with the voids in my life that had never gone away, just covered for a time. It was like waking up after a long nap. Only the waking up brought with it a fresh wave of desperation.

The hole in my heart had become cavernous.

The resentment blossomed into unreasonable hatred towards the man I was married to. It wasn't because of his treatment of me; it was born out of the deep hatred I had towards myself. I had nothing to give him because I was an empty well. I couldn't receive from him because I felt so unworthy of being loved. It was the perfect storm as they say.

Even more than all of that, I missed God's presence in my life. Again, words are so shallow to describe how lonely I was for Him.

In the rare times that I would let myself dream, I dreamt of once again being able to feel His closeness, to hear His Voice. I longed for those arms to wrap themselves around me and pull me into His embrace.

But those dreams would quickly be shattered by my shame.

I felt so unworthy of Him.

He had never shown me anything but goodness and kindness. I had repaid Him with my betrayal and sin.

I fully accepted there was no more hope for me. There was only the constant shroud of shame that covered me and buried me in an inky stench. I couldn't stand being with me. I hated the person I had become.

I was tired. The bone-weary kind of tired that drove me to more bad decisions. I didn't want to continue living with a man I didn't love and knew I couldn't love.

I filed for a divorce.

I was running again.

CHAPTER 8:

THROUGH THE EYES OF A CHILD

Searching for acceptance is a cruel taskmaster. It drives us to places we never intended to go and causes us to do things beyond our own moral compass.

In the course of this agonizing time of separation and divorce, I met a guy who had fallen in love with my child. He liked me alright, but he was enamored with my daughter.

I no longer had the illusion I would find love. Not the real kind of love my heart craved. I convinced myself it didn't exist except in dime store novels, and I was a fool trying to find it in the real world.

I was a mother now, and it was time to let go of childhood fantasies and grow up. My daughter needed me.

This man was coming out of serious drug addictions and alcohol abuse. He realized the hard way that living the wild life wasn't all it claimed to be. We both were ready to get out of Dodge. Once again, I found my ticket out of town, and I was on the run.

He was escaping from old friends, family pressure, and addictions. I was fleeing bad memories, tormenting thoughts, and myself. We packed our things, and the three of us moved to Illinois.

It wasn't a love-filled romantic relationship. It was a mutual understanding that we both were disillusioned with life. Together, we agreed to create our own standard of happiness.

It was nice to have a guy in my life to share the load, share expenses, have some fun, and he was good to my daughter. There were no long-term expectations. We were friends with benefits, set on finding our own version of the American dream.

After our move, the need for me to finally go back to work was apparent. We had a newly established business, which was growing, but not able to fully support us yet.

After a great deal of searching, I found a daycare with an opening. It was located at the local First Baptist church and had great reviews.

It tore me up inside to leave my precious daughter there. She was only 2 years old. I still needed her to need me.

She, on the other hand, never looked back. She loved the interaction with other kids and stole the hearts of everyone who met her.

In the weeks following, she would come home from her school singing. That was her favorite past time, next to reading. Her list of songs included "Jesus Loves Me" and "The B-I-B-L-E" complete with hand motions.

Her beautiful voice singing so sweetly quickened my heart. I was humbled by the genuine love my sweet child had for God. She seemed to dance in the realm of His loving care that I had once known.

It heightened my own despair. At times it seemed the chasm in my soul would swallow me up.

In the darkest parts of the night, when the emptiness would come crashing down on me, I would go into her room and watch her sleeping peacefully. She was a beautiful little girl with such innocence and purity.

I felt so unworthy of being her mother. I longed to keep her from all the hurts I had known. I was very protective of her, and cautious at all times of who she was with.

On this night, sitting on the bed and looking at her cherub face, I remembered the night I spent on the hay many years before. In this current place and time beside her, I began again to understand the gentle sounds that momma cow made to bring comfort to its fearful newborn calf.

My heart ached to provide the same comfort and love to this child. I wanted to be to her everything I had never known.

I just didn't know how.

The desire to give her something in life that was solid and secure was my driving force.

Maybe, for my daughter's sake, I could take the risk of trying to find my way back to God. I wasn't confident He would hear me, but the God I remembered would not reject this beautiful little girl with such a love for Him.

She had not disappointed Him. I had.

In the twilight glow, I sat and wondered to myself. How does one go about finding God after you had walked away from Him?

CHAPTER 9:

PANIC AND THE PASTOR

One afternoon, I had taken my daughter to her gymnastics class at the YMCA. I was sitting in the lobby looking at the paper when I spotted an ad for a "Christian and Missionary Alliance" church.

I had no clue what it meant, but the emblem in their ad caught my attention. With nothing else to go on, that was my guiding star. Maybe this was the best course of action on my new journey to find God.

As quickly as the thought came, old fear tried to crowd in, but a new determination washed over me. I was not going to fail my daughter.

She would have what she needed. One thing I was sure of, she needed God in her life.

We visited the next Sunday.

Surprisingly, it was a pleasant experience. The pastor seemed friendly. The people were nice but not smothering. That was important because I wanted to be able to slip in and slip out quickly. However, that was impossible, since my daughter made her presence known with her friendly chatter all the way out the door.

Later that week, the pastor's wife called to ask if I would be interested in having them stop by. I heard my mouth saying, "Yes, that would be nice," as my brain was shouting at me, "What are you doing?"

We set a time for later that week. Did I really just agree to that?

As the day approached, panic set in. I was nearly paralyzed with fear. What was I thinking when I said they could actually come to my house?

As my thoughts raced, I fully expected them to reject me once they stepped foot in my home. There was no denying that I was no longer church material. I'm not sure what I thought that meant, but whatever it was, it wasn't me.

The lie had embedded itself deeply in me that I didn't measure up to Christian standards. I had failed God miserably when all He had ever shown me was kindness.

I prepared myself for a good chewing out. Soon I had convinced myself they were coming to ask me not to come back to their church again. They wouldn't want me to taint their people or their reputation in the community, they would say.

On and on it went until the day of their visit arrived. I was a wreck. My feelings of unworthiness seemed to be paramount. I burnt the cookies I tried to bake. I went to bake a cake and had no eggs. Everything I tried to do to make their visit pleasant failed.

Finally, I decided it wasn't worth all this pain. I tried to call and cancel. No answer. This was long before the days of cell phones.

I frantically tried again.

No answer.

The minutes ticked by. Should I just leave? I could say something came up. Can you lie to a pastor? What's wrong with me? The thoughts thundered through my brain in rapid-fire succession.

The battle in my heart raged even more loudly. Get out now while you can and spare yourself the pain! In the midst of my angst, I didn't realize time was passing quickly.

I heard the knock on my door, and my heart dropped in fear. Too late to run.

Just get through this, and you don't ever have to see them again. You got this! Calm down. Keep it brief and stay on safe ground. Get them out the door as quickly as you can, I coached my frazzled mind.

Somehow, I managed to open the door. I may have smiled. They politely entered and sat down. We chatted awkwardly. They seemed to sense my discomfort.

The wife was sweet and genuinely caring. To my amazement, she had brought a loaf of banana bread. She didn't have a fake smile fixed in place. She seemed authentic and engaged. This was odd to me and disarming.

The pastor was very kind. When he sat down, he settled in, like he was at home. He didn't perch on the edge of his seat in a distant kind of way like I was. He was relaxed and fatherly. He asked good questions but wasn't nosey. He seemed to be interested in me as a person.

However, there was something about his eyes that I found unnerving. I found it hard to keep his gaze, and I kept looking away. When we did make eye contact, it was like he saw right into me. I didn't see judgment from him; just wisdom and peace.

They both were gracious. Did they know all I really wanted was for them to leave quickly?

Thankfully, they were keeping the visit short and started to gather their things. We all stood up as they headed towards the door.

Relief flooded over me.

The pastor paused, and respectfully asked if he could pray before they took off. It seemed like a normal thing for pastorally people to do. I dutifully bowed my head.

As this pastor prayed, it was like an electric shock ran through me. This guy talked to God like he was really talking to somebody he *knew*.

It was like you would talk to an intimate friend. He made it seem that God was right there with us in that very room.

The presence I felt when this man prayed was the same presence I felt holding me close all those years ago. My heart was racing.

The prayer ended, and still, I stood there, dazed. They moved out on the front porch and were graciously thanking me for welcoming them into my home. I was still trying to figure out the presence embracing me.

Then, it happened.

The pastor looked at me with those piercing but gentle eyes. He hesitated a moment and then said, "This doesn't usually happen with folks I've met for the first time, but as I was praying, the Lord spoke to me....."

I couldn't believe what I was hearing. Now I truly was in a panic. I instantly felt naked and vulnerable. I felt like my whole life was being examined and exposed right here, right now. I had come so close to escaping their cutting words, but here it was.

My perception had been right. Those eyes of his had really looked into my soul, and now I was in for it!

I braced myself for the judgment I knew was about to fall hard. There was no more running. God had found me, and this man was going to let me have it! I was terrified!

His voice came firm and strong, "...He wants you to know He knows everything about you; all you've done, and all you've endured, and He loves you more than you will ever understand. He wants you to come home to Him."
He paused and said, "God wants me to tell you He was there all the

time."

The Pastor's wife gave me a quick hug before walking to their car.

After closing the door, I ran to my bedroom, pulled open a bottom drawer of my dresser and grabbed the worm out Bible I'd gotten for my 12th birthday. I headed to our basement. My mind was racing.

After all my failures; my betrayal, the disappointment I was to Him, the sin and the years I ran out of my guilt and shame, could God really love me?

CHAPTER 10:

FLOODGATES OPEN

I sat on those basement steps and spent the next 7 hours pouring out my heart and soul to the God I had longed to know since I was a little girl. As bitter tears poured down my face, my life played like a movie unfolding before me.

I grieved over my sin and all the bad choices I had made. I was in sorrow seeing the hurt I caused people, the pain I inflicted on others. I was humbled to see my pride, selfishness, and stubborn heart that had kept me in a dark place for so long.

Gut-wrenching sobs came from deep places within me. My cries of repentance, recounting the many ways I had failed Him and sinned against His holiness, poured out of my mouth like a torrent.

My heart agonized over the hurt, the abuse, the rejection, and the abandonment I had experienced. The physical and emotional pain of those dark days came back hard. I stayed in that place until there was simply nothing left to say.

Somehow, out of the depths of my sorrow, I knew it was true. God loves me!

I could barely grasp the thought. It was flittering through my mind, weaving its way to expose and unravel the many lies I had believed about Him and about myself for a long time. I was startled to hear me saying it out loud. I needed to hear the words and grab them tightly, clinging to them as my lifeline.

God loves me!

The realization kept washing over my wounded and deeply broken heart. I felt those very familiar arms hold me closer than I had ever experienced before. His peace came. It poured over me and filled the dry, empty places.

I never wanted to leave this place, resting in His embrace and basking in His love.

I was on an entirely new path I had never walked before. I needed help navigating through these waters.

With that understanding, I did something I had not risked since a small child. I asked for help.

First thing the next morning, I called the pastor. After I explained what had happened to me in the basement, I asked if he and his wife would be willing to talk with me. I needed help understanding what this all meant.

They invited me over.

When I arrived, they received me with great love and compassion. She held me in her arms, letting me blubber and snot all over the place. For the first time in my life, I verbally poured out all of the hurts I had held inside for a very long time.

They spent a great deal of time speaking with me, explaining Bible things and answering my questions with tender love and patience.

Pastor Wayne opened up his Bible and began showing me what had happened on those basement stairs. It had a name, and he wanted me to understand from the Word of God what it was.

It's called salvation through repentance. Repentance, he went on to explain, was our sorrowful confession of sin. Confession is simply telling God what we had done with no excuses for our sin, no blaming anyone else and not trying to justify it. We must own what we have done in the presence of a Holy God, laying it at the foot of the cross and accepting all Jesus has done to redeem us out of darkness.

That day, I knew beyond any doubt that the Jesus story I had read all those years was not some distant historical event. It wasn't random, impersonal, or generic. It was so much more than the manger scene we're all so familiar with.

No, I saw Jesus' birth, death, and resurrection was an act of God reaching into my own personal world. Jesus had come to die and lived again so He could save *me*. His story was forever a part of my story. My story began with Him before the foundations of the world were laid. He knew me then, and He called me to be His own.

The next thing I heard was, "He was the One who held you close as a small child when you were being abused, He was the one who rode with you through the mountains and sang songs to you in the rivers. He was the One who defended and protected you from the demons that repeatedly tried to kill you after they marked you for destruction. He was the One you cried out to in the barn. He was the One who never let you go. His Name is Jesus, and He died for you because He loves you so much."

The hunger in my heart to know God had led me to this time and this place.

The answer to my question from years ago, "Could it ever be?" was given.

Yes, the love I had seen between that momma cow and her calf could be mine!

And now it was.

43

I had come home to His love.

CHAPTER 11:

WAYNE AND DEANNA

If ever there was a honeymoon phase of my life, I was living it. The days were sweet, the sun shone brighter than I ever remembered, and the flowers this spring were more beautiful than I could describe. My heart had found rest, and there was joy in my step.

During this time, there was another new beginning for me. I was experiencing one of the most beautiful friendships I have known in my life.

I didn't know it was possible to love people as much as I loved Pastor A. Wayne Glover and his sweet wife, Deanna. Not having strong physical or emotional connections with my natural family, this amazing couple took me under their wings and became family to me.

They not only nurtured and discipled my faith; they taught me how to do life. Deanna taught me how to cook, shared recipes with me, and taught me how to make jelly. She helped me organize my home, taught me basic household things like how to sort laundry, ways of cleaning I hadn't known, and basics of sewing. She shared all those motherly household tips that were sorely lacking in my life.

She was there for the births of my next three children, took care of me when I was sick, and held me up when times were hard. There is rarely a day that goes by when I do not reflect on something she taught me in those sweet years. To this day, her potato roll recipe is a family favorite.

Likewise, Pastor Wayne was a source of fatherly stability to me. He gave me counsel, taught me how to draw from God's wisdom and draw close to Him. Most importantly for me, he restored my ability to trust a man.

I treasured the fact that Pastor Wayne loved me enough to say the hard things, and give correction as needed. He was the iron that sharpens iron in my life for many years. He is one of God's true Shepherds.

I wasn't easy to love in those early days, either.

Have you ever noticed how our sweet babies we love so dearly throw up on you, poop on you, burp loudly, and can be rather demanding of your time?

Then, just when you think they've outgrown that phase and life is good, they enter those toddler stages. Those tiny tykes are totally unpredictable. They don't have filters to know things that should or should not be said in public. They will, for sure, embarrass you.

Their curiosity gets them into things they ought not to get into. Their questions are endless, and no answer seems like enough for them. They're striving for independence and want to do it themselves, which causes them to make mistakes we saw coming. Those are trying years while we wait for them to mature.

Well, it's not so different in God's family.

I was that baby in an adult body. I was not church-trained and was immature in many ways!

Sunday after Sunday, I was listening, consuming really, the messages Pastor Wayne taught. I was like a young woman who had been lost in the desert without water and near certain death when I happened to stumble into an oasis.

Pastor Wayne held out this incredible relationship with Jesus as Savior, Lord, Master, King, Father, and Friend. When he taught the Word of God, he made it very clear that Jesus was concerned about every aspect of our lives.

This resonated deeply within me.

I remembered the day my horse dumped me in the orchard, and I lay there, unable to move. The warmth that came and surged through my body I now realized was His healing touch. He was restoring me and enabling me to get back up and ride home.

Recollecting when the old man fell on top of me, fondling my breasts, I remembered the Voice telling me to, "Get out!" In the panic of the situation, He had cleared my thoughts and given me the physical strength to get out from underneath him and run home.

As Pastor Wayne continued to teach, both from the pulpit and in the many hours I peppered him with my questions, the things I had read in the Bible years ago began to fall into place in my understanding. The ragged pieces of my life were falling into some order, and I was seeing myself more clearly.

It seemed for a long while that there were daily things brought to my mind requiring repentance. My heart was being tilled, the weeds and rocks removed, and the soil made soft and ready to receive new seed. This was the work Pastor Wayne and Deanna walked me through. Even when they didn't see immediate results, they were faithful to God and faithful to me in speaking Truth.

Many of those seeds would not fully come to fruition until years later. Some have now grown into towering oaks, with deep roots drawing from God's springs. Others are just now being watered, and little sprouts continue to spring up.

It takes a powerful love, mixed generously with patience, gentleness and long-suffering to walk spiritual babies through those infant and toddler years into a place of maturity. This is a spiritual relationship, requiring wisdom and grace, strength and tenderness, toughness and guidance. They gave me all those things freely and fully.

I'm sure they wondered many times if I would ever grow up...and they loved me through it all!

I was messed up.

The depth of my mess was yet to be revealed.

CHAPTER 12:

FACING THE DARKNESS

It seems like it should be easy to rest in God's love, right? I was surrounded by people who loved me. There was great Bible teaching. My baby faith was slowly taking hold.

Yet in the midst of it all, there was a battle raging inside my heart.

I was tormented by horrible dreams almost nightly from when I was a child. These dreams were highly disturbing and sexual in nature. Abusive, evil, nasty, sexual dreams that left me shaken.

The dreams also left me feeling dirty, damaged, and like a second-class Christian.

I noticed when I was outside my home, even with my children, that men, not good men, were attracted to me. The looks in their eyes brought terror to my heart. Many tried to make lewd advances or sexual comments that were rude and obnoxious.

What was wrong with me? What was I doing to attract their attention?

I had such a sense of God's love for me, yet fear of everything was my constant companion. It was like a constant tug of war for my peace.

Even though I felt very close to Pastor Wayne and Deanna, I didn't have the same relationships with other people within their church. I often felt like an outsider. I couldn't relate to their stories, nor could they relate to mine. Largely, I wasn't willing to share my past with people.

When asked how I first became aware of God, how could I tell them it was from a momma cow and her new calf in a barn at the age of 10? These were people who had spent their whole lives in a church setting, and were proud to be third and fourth generation followers of Jesus who never so much as said a bad word.

What would they think of me and my far-from-perfect childhood?

Theirs was a story of preservation from the evil of this world, they said. Mine a story of redemption from the midst of its grasp. I would have loved to have their story, and I began comparing myself to them. Every time I went around that barn, I felt second-rate.

I believed God loved me, but I wasn't convinced He loved me as much as He loved other Christians. These thoughts fed my feelings of inferiority.

Rather than be encouraged, I felt small and intimidated when I listened to the glowing testimonies of long years of seamlessly walking with God. Every story of victories won was like a noose around my struggling heart.

I was ashamed of my story.

I struggled with telling the truth; at least the whole truth. From my childhood, I had accepted my grandmother's and my mother's words spoken over me, declaring me a liar. In time, lying became a learned pattern. My intent was not to be dishonest; it was to hide. If you tell people what they want to hear, you don't get hurt. If I agreed with those in authority over me, even when it was wrong, I wouldn't be screamed at or punished.

Now I understood that lying was not God's desire for my life. He deals in truth, and He calls His people to also live in His Truth.

There was a wrestling in me I didn't understand. I tried to stop these things, but I was not able to overcome them, which added to my shame. I felt phony, and began to doubt myself. In time, I questioned if my salvation was real.

These were dark, secret, hidden things. But I knew.

And I was acutely aware that God knew.

Why couldn't I be free?

I tossed and turned in my misery for what seemed like a lifetime. In reality, it was a few weeks.

Finally, worn out, beaten up, and overwhelmed by my failure, I humbled my heart and ran home to the only place I knew would be safe. I asked my Heavenly Father for help, and He lovingly met me in my trouble. He directed me back to Pastor Wayne and Deanna.

They greeted me with the same love they had extended to me time and time again. They sat patiently as I poured out the ugliness in me, never flinching or backing away from the ick. In my childlike way, I held nothing back.

Feeling very vulnerable and expecting their rejection, they held me as I wept bitterly. I was horrified at the things I was saying, but they lovingly reminded me of who I am in Christ. They didn't seem surprised at all about this battle in me.

To me, it felt like I was being ripped in two from the inside out. I began to wonder if they had heard what I had said, because they were very calm and peaceful.

Pastor Wayne looked at me with those piercing eyes and gently said, "We've been waiting for this."

He went on to explain that when God met me on those basement steps, He took the burden and penalty of my sin. Indeed, the law of sin was broken off of me. In that moment, He filled me with His Holy Spirit, and

I now had His power living in me.

This was the beginning of my journey, and there was so much more to know.

"It is time," Pastor Wayne said, "for you to grow in your understanding of God's Kingdom. Jesus didn't die only to save you from your sins. He died so you could be made whole and bring His Kingdom from heaven to earth."

When he said those words "made whole," hope rose up within me.

In that moment, I realized that I needed to come face to face with my brokenness. My sin had been remedied, but the ugly wounds within me needed the healing touch only Jesus could bring.

I had no idea what this meant, but I wanted to be made whole.

I was ready to face my wounds.

CHAPTER 13:

TWO KINGDOMS

Since meeting Pastor Wayne and Deanna, I was fascinated, watching them be used of God to bring freedom to many lives. Not just in the church through His teaching, but also in the community. Many people who didn't attend any church came to them for counseling to become free.

Even though I saw it, I lacked understanding how this freedom was gained.

What I hadn't fully understood in those years was the call on their lives to set the captives free. They had been gifted by God with a deliverance ministry.

Now, as I sat in their office hearing these words spoken to me, I had no idea what that even was. As I listened to them share their heart, I began to see them in an entirely new light.

As I heard their words, I realized they understood, with great discernment and clarity, the forces of darkness that run rampant in the world. Having seen many lives utterly destroyed by these evil forces, their hearts were moved in compassion to bring God's Truth to bear on each person who came to them for help.

They walked in confident assurance of the victory we have to overcome every enemy through the shed Blood of Jesus. They were unwavering in the battle over those who had been deceived, and those who had suffered great harm at the hand of dark powers.

I was even more honored and thankful to have them in my life. I'm telling you, these are the kind of people you want in your corner when the battle is raging as it was in me.

Pastor Wayne began to show me in the Word of God about this battle. He sent me home with several scriptures to study and hear what God had to say about this.

As I studied the scriptures, I started seeing with greater clarity the two kingdoms in operation in all of our lives. I had read about them many times, but not with understanding.

One Kingdom was ruled and reigned over by the loving hand of God. It was filled with Himself in all Light, beauty, and His love. It is His, ruled by His hand in Truth and righteousness. This Kingdom functions as a banner to all who are walking with Him, yielded and surrendered to His will above their own.

When we are walking in His Kingdom, the fruit of His Spirit fills the hearts of His people with goodness, kindness, joy, peace, and many other wonderful things. He is the Father of Life.

The other kingdom was ruled by an evil force that hates the Kingdom of God. This kingdom is filled with rebellion, hate, witchcraft, bitterness, and deception. This fruit is also made known in the hearts of its followers. Some are very good at covering these evil things, but the hidden things are always revealed in time. This kingdom was driven by the father of death.

As I continued to study the scriptures, I saw clearly the battle doesn't end when you are saved. The battle actually begins in earnest.

Before we were saved, we already belonged to the kingdom of darkness. The enemy's only job was to keep us in the darkness by wrapping chain upon chain around us. We weren't any threat to him, and with little effort, we were easily controlled through our addictions, wounds, bitterness, and hatred, just to name a few of the evil tricks of his dark trade.

Once we meet Jesus and break free from the law of sin and death, those chains are unlocked, and their power to hold us is broken. The enemy knows this better than we do, at first. He blinds our eyes to this truth, so we walk around with the heaviness of our chains, which impedes our growth and steals our freedom. He knows full well the locks have been broken, and there is nothing holding these chains up, except the lies we believe.

All of a sudden, I realized what it meant in the Bible when we're told that after we've been saved, we were transferred from the kingdom of darkness into the Kingdom of Light. It's literally changing our citizenship!

The problem is, the rulers of darkness don't want to let the people go. Once we are saved, the enemy goes into "red alert" and works double time to thwart us at every turn. He and his evil cronies work feverishly to bring death and destruction to those who escape his clutches through salvation.

If he can't keep us from the Kingdom of God, he works hard to keep us bound up with anything he can get his evil talons into. He uses our past sins to condemn us, even though he knows we have been forgiven. After all, he is the father of lies, so lying is a logical means for him to use.

He accuses us when we fall, telling us we're not really saved; that we'll never measure up to God's standards, and he tries to get us to throw up our hands and quit. His whole purpose is to keep us ignorant of his plans, so we remain spiritual babies -immature and ineffective.

This was all news to me! I didn't know the enemy had devised evil schemes, laid traps for my feet, and knew much about me that he could use to try and stop me.

Our enemy does not want us to know who we are in Jesus. He doesn't want us walking in the power Jesus won for us to conquer every work of darkness. He wants us ignorant to the Truth that in the resurrection power of Jesus Christ, we can be a considerable threat to the evil plans of darkness.

The enemy lives to rob, kill, and destroy the faith we now have in Jesus Christ, and the freedom He bought for us with His own blood.

If the enemy succeeds, he will prevent us from fulfilling our God-given destiny now.

As Pastor Wayne, Deanna, and I continued to talk of these things and I searched the scriptures, my eyes were being opened to this battle taking place all around us. It was also opening my eyes to the personal battle taking place within my own soul.

Two different kingdoms. Two opposing purposes.

One filled with God, who gave His Son to redeem me from the power of darkness and restore to me the gift of an eternal relationship with Him beginning now.

The other filled with an enemy who wanted to keep me in deception and lead me to eternal death separated from God forever.

God wanted me whole, set free to walk victoriously, bearing His Name.

The enemy wanted me utterly destroyed.

I began seeing my childhood through different eyes.

The pain, the suffering, the accusations, and the struggles that drove me here tonight took on new meaning. I didn't have complete understanding, but one thing I knew for certain, I wanted nothing to do with the kingdom of darkness.

I knew it was going to be painful to face my brokenness. But I was determined to have the freedom that was rightfully mine as a child of the living God!

I bowed my head and said to God, "Regardless of the cost, I want to be free. Show me how!"

Nancy Z. Everist

CHAPTER 14:

PREPARING FOR BATTLE

After I had done a thorough study of what the scriptures had to say about all of this, I met with Pastor Wayne and Deanna again. I felt like a soldier showing up for basic training. I knew nothing about how to fight this battle, but I had a deep hunger to learn it all. I wanted to be equipped to fight well.

Pastor Wayne was being mindful in laying a solid foundation of Truth. He didn't just hand me a sword and turn me loose, which would have been disastrous on so many levels. No, he began by mentoring me about my authority as a blood-bought believer in Jesus Christ.

"You can't go into enemy territory to take back ground if there's any doubt in your mind Who your King is and for which Kingdom you are fighting. He is the One sending you into battle," he counseled. "When you know He's directing your path, you can face anything, because He is faithful who has promised never to leave or forsake you."

Day by day, we met. As they imparted Truth to me, they bathed me in prayer. They answered my gazillion questions, and they stood in the place of protection over me. I didn't understand what "standing in the gap" meant back then, but I've come to learn that without their faithful intercession, it is doubtful I would have made it through.

"Never forget," Pastor Wayne continued, "You're not going into battle in your own strength or with your own motives. You are being sent to take back what is rightfully yours because of what Jesus won for you through His death, burial, and resurrection."

In this conversation, it was my heart he was referring to.

Since early childhood, the enemy had stolen many things right out of my heart. My innocence, my ability to feel safe, fatherly affirmations of worth, the wonder and joy of being a child, to name only a few.

As I gained knowledge in the scriptures, I was seeing my personal need for deliverance. I needed their help in this battle to regain those lost things. When I talked with them about this, we set aside time to fast and pray.

They were seeking direction from God.

I was asking God to give me courage.

We agreed to meet the following week.

I really had no idea what deliverance looked like. I understood the concept in vague terms but wasn't sure what to expect.

Up to now, the only time I had even heard the words was when my sister was studying to be a witch and went to watch "The Exorcist." When she returned from watching that movie, she was graphic in her descriptions. It terrified me at the time, as it was doing again now.

Fear was permeating my thoughts. I felt paralyzed by it. I began having nightmares for which there are no words to describe.

Horrible thoughts assaulted my mind about Pastor Wayne and Deanna. All of a sudden, I wondered if they were really good people. Maybe they were actually out to deceive me. Maybe they were going to get me alone and kill me!

I couldn't eat, I couldn't sleep.

I jumped at every sound, and was scared of the dark.

I was a wreck!

After four days of this, I decided it wasn't worth it. I would be fine as I was. People lived with nightmares and horrible thoughts all the time. I just needed to grow up, grab myself by the bootstraps, and cowgirl up.

I missed a meeting with Pastor Wayne and didn't answer Deanna's calls. That Sunday, I skipped church. I was home, trying to hide. Terror had taken up residence in my home and was surrounding me. I had no idea what, but there was something out there, I just knew it. Something very evil and very determined to hurt me. I didn't feel safe anywhere.

On the fifth morning, there was a knock on my door. I opened it to find Pastor Wayne and Deanna standing there. It was a relief to see them. They were like rocks I could anchor to, and I was ashamed I had been avoiding them.

He looked at me and said, "We've been praying for you. God has revealed to us how the enemy is lying to you and causing great fear."

He went on to tell me the things I had been fighting over the past several days. I hadn't said anything to them, but they were spot on!

They told me how God woke them up through the nights, calling them to pray and fight over me. As they shared these things with me, it was like a cold rod was rammed down my spine.

Suddenly, I knew how real the battle is. Up to that point, I had believed it in my head. This was different. Now, it was real. It was in front of me, surrounding me. I could tangibly feel the presence of evil. It took me back to places in my childhood that were painful to visit.

The enemy had overplayed his hand.

Once again, I fell into their arms weeping, and asked their forgiveness for running from them. They held me close and prayed. As they prayed over me, the lying voices stopped, the fear was pushed back, and sweet peace filled my heart.

No longer did I doubt the lengths the enemy would go to in keeping me in bondage. The darkness that settled on me those past few days served like gas on the flames of my desire to be free. I was tired of being a pawn in the enemy's hand, and taking all the blows he wanted to deal out at his whim.

When we finished praying, I was sobered, as a new courage and resolve rose up within me. This ancient war between these two kingdoms had landed on my doorstep.

It was time for me to rise up and take my part in it.

I was back in business.

Game on.

CHAPTER 15:

ARMOR UP

Arriving at Wayne's office, he and Deanna greeted me warmly. I was nervous, but I was more tired of being beaten up every day by the torment and lies I was experiencing.

Before this meeting, the three of us had met many times. They had given me a lengthy questionnaire to fill out, which was very thorough. It brought to memory things I had not thought about in years, nor would I have considered them significant enough to share.

Some of the questions were about family history. I didn't have the answers, so I called my mother in Oregon for details. I learned things about both sides of my family that I had never known, nor would I have asked about before. She wasn't always forthcoming with family things, especially as it pertained to my natural father, but it was still helpful. I'm sure those were uncomfortable conversations for her as well.

Pastor Wayne had reviewed the questionnaire before this meeting and sought God's direction for this time. I looked into their faces for reassurance, and their warm smiles were welcoming. We all took our places.

Pastor Wayne began with prayer, which was exactly what I needed in that moment. We had prayed often together over the past several months, and it was a familiar place to rest. It was a natural beginning for a spiritual work.

That he prayed was no surprise, but how he prayed was very different. These were prayers of a man in authority, taking dominion over this time, and consecrating it to the King of all kings.

We all had spent the day before asking God to reveal any known sin in our lives. If there were things Holy Spirit brought to mind, we repented of them so we could enter into this time with clean hands and pure hearts through the Blood of Jesus. Even still, Pastor Wayne asked again for Holy Spirit to test and try us in those inward parts only He knows. He invited Holy Spirit to have free reign in our hearts and minds, and to fill us as He filled the place we had gathered.

I've said this several times before, but there's no other way for me to explain the presence of God. For me, it's as if He comes and picks me up in His arms and holds my head against His chest. His heartbeat brings me great comfort and strength. His arms provide protection, and it's the safest place I know. From His heart, pure love flows and washes over me.

It was from this place we moved forward, in believing faith, that He was guiding our steps.

Pastor Wayne began praying protection and covering over each one of us. I felt those arms tighten, and I knew regardless of what the day would hold, I was secure in God.

He continued by praying the armor of God upon us. I had read about God's armor in the Bible, but I hadn't thought about it as something real in my life for today. I was enthralled and drawn in as he continued.

He prayed the Helmet of Salvation, asking for Holy Spirit to give us the mind of Jesus Christ. He took our thoughts captive unto obedience to the Word of God that nothing would be accepted as true if it didn't line up with the Bible. He prayed for Holy Spirit to protect our minds from the deceit of the enemy.

I hadn't heard anything like this before. I didn't realize the scriptures about these pieces of armor were actually real for me today. I always thought of them as great stories from another time. Yet as he prayed this armor on, somehow, I felt bolder and stronger.

The Breastplate of Righteousness. He asked Holy Spirit to cover us under the righteousness of Jesus Christ. We acknowledged our need for Him as our Savior, knowing apart from Him, we have nothing and can do nothing, but in Him we have been given all power and authority.

The Girdle of Truth. He continued by asking Holy Spirit to bring only His Truth. He asked for every lie of the enemy to be revealed, torn down and cast away forever. He said we earnestly were seeking for His Truth to reign in our innermost being, in the deepest part of us.

At this, I started weeping. Oh, how I longed to walk only in Truth. Shame tried to rise up and knock me off my chair, but love was holding me fast.

Wasn't this why I was here? To be set free? I wasn't about to give up now.

I was drawn back to Pastor Wayne's prayer.

"Shod our feet with the preparation of the Gospel of Peace." He asked for peace that passes our understanding, our natural mind. The peace that only God can give, peace that comes from Jesus, the Prince of Peace. He also prayed that every enemy that is trying to steal peace or corrupt it would be trampled under our feet.

"The Shield of Faith." He asked Holy Spirit to bring His divine protection as we stood steadfast behind the shield of faith, believing all that was written in the Word of God were His promises to us, real and relevant to our daily lives. By faith in Who He is and believing He is faithful who has promised, Pastor Wayne declared that every fiery dart, every lie, every wicked plan of the enemy would be completely extinguished and cast away.

Then he prayed we would pick up the Sword of the Spirit - the Word of God. That everything that was said, done, thought, and believed would be tested and tried through God's precious Word to us. The Bible gave us our standard for living, empowering us to slice through the darkness and bring Light and Life by His Truth.

I sat dumbfounded. Completely speechless.

I don't know how else to describe this, but as he prayed, I felt like I was completely surrounded by a thousand glowing angels in full battle armor with gleaming swords drawn ready to battle for me. They were standing in a circle around that place, forming a barrier impenetrable by any enemy.

Personally, I felt small. I was so humbled by this display of power on my behalf. I wanted to crawl under my chair, knowing I wasn't worthy of their presence because I was very aware there were things in me that were not holy. I was afraid to look at them, so sure I would see disgust and disdain.

With my head hung and shoulders slumped, I felt a hand on my shoulder. Somehow, I knew it wasn't Pastor Wayne or Deanna. I looked up into the face of the largest angel, and what I saw caused me to cry hard.

In his eyes, I saw approval.

In the depths of my spirit, I heard him speak, "Be strong, little one and take courage. You are not alone."

From this place, the work began.

CHAPTER 16:

OUR ENEMY FIGHTS DIRTY

We all sat there in this holy moment, savoring the presence of the Kingdom of the Living God as it touches earth. I had never experienced such peace and power in the same moment before. I wasn't sure what I had expected, but this certainly was not it!

After a time, Pastor Wayne looked at me and said, "This time we're entering into isn't just about you being set free, it's about training you as a warrior for the Kingdom of God. This may be a bit different because there are things you need to see and understand that will serve you well for the rest of your life." I had the utmost respect for this man of God, and I paid attention.

He went on to explain to me some of the ways the enemy works.

"He ruthlessly attacks children," he explained. "He is constantly circling children, watching, waiting for an opportune time to bring great harm to them in the cruelest fashion possible."

Children are trusting and have the capacity to grasp spiritual truth far greater than adults because they've not yet been taught to doubt. They simply receive, trust, and believe. This is the great value of childlike faith; it is pure.

If the enemy can find a way to harm them, he can steal their childhood from them. From there, he begins to pour in the lies. He whispers to them his poison telling them they are not safe, nobody can be trusted, the world is dangerous, you are not lovable, you're all alone and on and on it goes.

Children accept and believe these lies because they line up with their experiences. Over time, these lies begin to form a stronghold and become their reality.

This can go many ways for each child, depending on their home life, their personality, and if they have praying people in their lives to cover them.

At best, they are deeply wounded and spend the rest of their lives looking for love, acceptance, and peace. At worst, they become adults who find comfort by harming others in the same ruthless manner.

As Pastor Wayne was sharing this with me, I was taken back to my own childhood. I could hear the many cruel things spoken over my life.

Nobody could ever love you.

You're damaged goods.

You're ugly - who would want you?!

You're fat.

My maternal grandmother accused me of being a liar when I ran home crying after escaping an old man trying to molest me. All because she was worried about her reputation in their small town.

My mother came to get me, but not to comfort me in my brokenness, rather to accuse. She would spend the rest of my growing up years re-enforcing to me I was a liar. It was easier for her than facing the truth in her own life.

You're to blame for all the bad things that ever happened in your home, your family, your life.

We are going to do you a favor and kill you to put you out of your misery.

You'll never be free of us; we own you!

I didn't realize I was speaking these things out loud until I heard Pastor Wayne say with a thundering voice, "In the Name of Jesus, you will be silent!"

You could hear a pin drop.

I looked up at him startled. By his voice, I thought I had made him angry at me. These were horrible things I said. Who does that?

He looked at me with such love and said, "Oh, precious girl, do you see how the enemy has been lying to you all your life?"

I had said those things to myself for so long I didn't recognize them as the lies they were. I truly believed them as truth, my truth.

"Those are lies; they are not true. Those aren't your thoughts; they are the thoughts the enemy has put into your mind and used other people to enforce over you," he continued. "Most importantly, these are certainly not God's thoughts towards you."

I sat there, soaking in those words. The Light of Truth was exposing the darkness.

He went on, "Hear me clearly. Those are lies from the enemy coming straight from the pit of hell. It was for your freedom that Jesus came and took away the power of the enemy to continue to torment you. Do you want to be free?"

I was sobbing so hard I could only nod my head. I had lived with these hateful voices for as long as I could remember to this very day. They had chased me, driven me, and run me into the ground. I had wrestled with them for way too long. I simply couldn't live under them any longer.

"This is the part where repentance comes in," Pastor Wayne continued. "Repentance breaks every chain the enemy tries to wrap around you."

Wait. What? Why did I need to repent?
As I listened, I felt anger rise up in me. It seemed unfair!

I was a child; they were the adults. They are the ones who had said these awful things to me. This is their fault, not mine. I said this out loud to Pastor Wayne and not nicely.

He met my anger with loving patience. He went on to say, "Yes, precious girl, you were victimized by the very people who should have loved and cared for you. The people you should have been able to trust."

Exactly. Now I was confused. Why did I need to repent again?

"You are repenting for believing the lies of the enemy. The lies that said you were anything less than what God Himself says you are. You are repenting to break off the agreement you made with the enemy, all those years ago, when you chose to embrace his lie. You have kept it alive in you and have fed it all these years by listening to what others think rather than what God says. Repentance is the key to be free from those lying spirits tormenting you," he explained.

When he said those words, I knew they were true. It was clear to me.

I literally fell out of my chair onto my knees. I hit the ground praying, crying out to God, asking forgiveness for believing those lying voices all those years.

As I was praying, I repented for the many times my hurt had driven me to accept lies. The very lies tormenting me each day of my life. My prayer of repentance was words mixed with a deep cry from places in me I didn't know existed.

My soul was yearning to have the roots of every lie yanked from the depths of my being. There was a physical ache in me to be free. I cried and prayed and sobbed when I saw what those lies had cost me.

Sometime during it all, Pastor Wayne and Deanna had slid to the floor beside me. Deanna was stroking my hair and singing very softly over me while Pastor Wayne was warring with the enemy who was fighting hard to keep me in bondage.

When I was spent, and there was nothing more to repent of, Pastor Wayne took my hands and looked into my eyes. He said, "Now is the time for you to use your authority as a believer in Jesus Christ and command the enemy to leave! He has no more legal right to stay because the sin that opened the door for him has been closed through repentance."

I wasn't sure how to say all that, but when I opened my mouth to pray, there was a surge of power rising up from my spirit, and the words came rushing out. I could sense a fierce battle taking place around me, sounding like swords crashing together. I knew those warring angels were fighting for me, and it gave me courage.

I commanded those demonic spirits to leave in Jesus' Name and declared that the Truth of Jesus Christ alone would reign in my life. I sensed the battle was won on my behalf, and sweet peace settled on my heart and in that room.

Pastor Wayne explained to me why the enemy had to leave. "Repentance broke the soul tie the enemy had. It shut the door he had opened to your soul through the harsh and cruel words he inflicted upon you as a child," he said.

"Now that the enemy has been routed," he said. "Let's ask Holy Spirit to fill that place with Himself."

Pastor Wayne led me in prayer, asking Holy Spirit to come and fill that place in me that was now clean and whole. He then prayed over me, asking Holy Spirit to teach me how to walk in the Truth of who I was.

He asked Holy Spirit to show me who I was in the Kingdom and to see myself through the Father's eyes. He prayed for protection and a guard over my mind with God's Truth.

I'm not sure there are enough words on this earth to explain the joy of having those chains fall off of me. It's like knowing you are drowning and having a hand reach down and pull you to the surface for a breath of fresh air.

I said to Pastor Wayne, "I wasn't the one lying. But I had believed them all."

Shaking my head, I softly said, "No more. I will be free."

Pastor Wayne explained it was important to be free of a lying spirit so we could move forward in Truth. We needed to move forward in deliverance with no doubts that what was spoken, revealed, or heard was now filtered through Truth. We weren't accepting any more of the enemy's lies.

I looked over from where I sat on the floor, and there was that angel. His chest was slightly heaving from battle, but there was a look of sure victory on his face. When our eyes met, he nodded to me, and there was a brief smile that spoke volumes to me.

I wasn't alone. We were doing this!

I got up off the floor, sat down in the chair, and looked at Pastor Wayne. Now that I knew what freedom felt like, I wanted it even more.

He saw my resolve, gave me a quick hug of encouragement, and took his place.

Once seated, he looked at me again, a question in his eyes.

"I'm okay," I said even though my voice was shaking. "I'm going to be strong. I'm not alone. So, what's next?"

CHAPTER 17:

ABSOLUTE EVIL

True to Pastor Wayne's word from the beginning, I was seeing things I hadn't seen before. I was also learning on my feet about the two kingdoms and the war that raged between them.

Before this time in my life, I'd heard it said if you're saved, you don't need to worry yourself about the enemy. "He was defeated at the cross, and all the battles are over", men would say. "The enemy is nothing to us anymore and we needn't bother ourselves with him because he was defeated."

The enemy was often presented as impish, maybe he caused a bit of childish mischief now and then, but not really evil. Actually, he even did some good now and then, some said. Others say if you just leave him alone, he'll leave you alone. Like a truce. One, of course, we can expect him to honor.

Movies took his image to various ends of the spectrum. He has been portrayed as everything from good witches, to a red-suited man with horns, a pitchfork and blood red eyes, all the way to making him out to be the stuff of your worst nightmares to get a thrill. A bit scary, but not terribly threatening in real life.

He isn't considered as intelligent as we are with our sophistication and advancements. We are encouraged to laugh and mock him but certainly not to concern ourselves about him.

Not much, anyway, if at all.

I saw quickly how wrong this is.

It's hard to grasp the existence of a being who is pure evil. Through and through. There's nothing good in him. Absolutely void of anything good.

100% E-V-I-L.

It baffles my mind to think about. It just doesn't compute in my reasoning, and my mind wants to reject it, spit it out because it's so far out of my realm of experience. I have to stop and slowly digest it; even then it is unfathomable.

As hard as it is to think of, there's no denying it.

Everything, and I do mean everything I was seeing and hearing in this room revealed more and more what this kingdom of darkness was about. I didn't know such depths of depravity, cruelty, debasement, and degradation were even possible. Until now.

The enemy is void of compassion. There's no kindness, no goodness, no human decency. He holds no respect for human life. He has no mercy. There is no appeal with him because he is void of morality. Reasoning with him is laughable, and he will turn and devour you.

To him, we are a target of abject and unbridled hatred. He quite literally can't stand the sight of us. Even those who choose to serve him, he despises with a bitter hatred. If we survive birth, which he works hard to make sure we don't; but if we do, he is relentless in his destruction of our lives.

In our strong sense of human decency, compounded by our inability to grasp the depths of evil he functions from, our mind is saying to us, "I've not done anything to him, why is he trying to kill me?"

Why? This is a valid question begging to be answered. As I studied the scriptures, I found God's answer.

Every man alive is created in the image of God. This is the very God the enemy abhors. This God, whose image we bear, is the Most High God who banished the enemy from his lofty estate, stripped him of his access to have authority in the Throne room and limited his powers.

The enemy was demoted, cast down, humiliated and his wrath turned to those who bear the image of the Great I Am. We are the living breathing physical reminder of the power of the King of all Kings and Lord of all Lord to whom the enemy lost everything.

As if that weren't enough, after creating man in His image, God gave man dominion to reign over the earth. The very kingdom our enemy called his own, God gave to man. This was cause for the enemy's hatred to build towards us, not because of anything we did. Simply because of Who our Creator is.

We are born into his crosshairs for destruction. Yet the evil in him desires we suffer great torment and torture before he utterly destroys us. This is his agenda for every person who draws their first breath.

Terrifying to me was seeing how relentless the enemy is for our destruction. Again, this is foreign to our minds that are rooted in compassion and respect for humanity.

Not so with the enemy of our souls. He comes at us and keeps coming and coming and coming again.

When you are down, he doesn't back off; he moves in to pounce. Hard. Kicks you again and again.

When you are tired, he sees your weakness and doubles up his forces to work harder to destroy you. Tirelessly. Driven by hate.

If you are sick, this is his moment, his opportunity to make your misery terminal. Torturous. Painful. Deadly.

He. Never. Stops.

He wears you down. He is set on grinding you into the dust and trampling you to pieces. He is absolutely relentless in his evil devices and schemes.

All those glib comments about him being impish and small, no longer able to bring us harm? All those things I previously thought I knew about the enemy? They are all lies.

Intelligent? It is beyond our ability to grasp how intellectual, tech-savvy, cunning, crafty, sly, deceitful, and masterful he is in scheming for our destruction.

He is the father of many scientific breakthroughs, as learned men yield their minds to him by tapping into supernatural power they do not understand, nor can they control. Men think they have discovered something new when all they have done is tap into an evil darkness that is age-old.

The enemy can do nothing without a man or woman operating as his surrendered agent to manifest his wickedness in the physical realm. We see this played out in history when men are deceived into believing the lies of the enemy. Men like Hitler, Stalin, and Mao would be examples of the enemy's evil incarnate in the flesh. These people, and many others like them to lesser degrees, are slaves to the enemy. He uses them and then discards them, to be eternally lost.

Even more diabolical, the longer he can prolong our agony; the more pain he can inflict and the deeper the wounds he can gouge into our souls, the more satisfaction he receives. He takes his evil accomplishments, and gloats before God.

He is a formidable foe. I had been clueless, but I was waking up to the Truth.

CHAPTER 18:

THE REAL JESUS

Likewise, before this time, my picture of Jesus was also pretty typical. My favorite depiction is of Jesus holding a baby lamb with little children gathered all around. Everyone is laughing and smiling, and all is well. This idyllic scene has always appealed to my little girl heart, starved for love and acceptance.

I loved the images of Jesus healing the sick, talking with the woman at the well, and teaching the people with great compassion in His eyes. Another favorite is of His baptism with the dove, and rays of glory falling from heaven on His head.

Each of these iconic images conjures up peace, kindness, compassion, joy and love. He is most certainly all those things, far above and beyond what we could ever dream of.

How grateful I am for the father heart of God, expressed in all Jesus did while He walked this earth. This boundless love drew my heart into trust and surrender to Him as my Lord, my Savior, and my King. While Jesus walked this earth, He was "Messiah Ben Joseph," the Suffering Servant, as the pure and spotless Lamb of God, slaughtered for the atonement of our sins.

I leaned on these tender, picturesque scenes of Jesus for comfort. They also defined who He was in my eyes.

They're not wrong. They're incomplete.

As I was being mercifully shaken out of my naïve understanding of the ruthless wickedness of the enemy, it was creating fear. I shared this with Pastor Wayne, and he asked me why I was afraid.

I paused, hung my head while thinking of my image of Jesus, and said, "I don't want Jesus to be hurt anymore for me."

He looked at me and said, "Jesus isn't limited by your small view of Him. Let Him show you Who He is!"

As He said those words, I looked over at the angel who was standing watch over us. It was like he grew before my eyes. He started to resonate and glow; His sword was shining so brightly it was hard to look at it, and His eyes were like liquid fire. He raised his hands and his sword as he looked up into heaven, and said in a voice that thundered, "Behold, the Captain of the Host!"

There was a roar, like a lion's roar, with lightning, thunder, rolling clouds that billowed like smoke and a sense of Light, power, and awe that pushed me to the ground, face down. The room filled with an essence of authority I had never known. Everything seemed to vibrate with His presence.

Without any words spoken, in that moment, I knew there was not any being who could ever stand against the Lion of Judah. There was no power greater, no wisdom above Him, no scheme He could not utterly shatter, and no enemy He could not defeat.

This was Jesus, the One who had conquered sin, death, and the grave. The One who took captivity captive and presented them before His Father. Jesus had fulfilled his role as Messiah Ben Joseph. He was now "Messiah Ben David, the Warring, Conquering King! "

I instantly realized my error. All this time, I had seen the enemy as the opposite of Jesus. Equal foes matched toe-to-toe. Counterparts.

This was completely wrong!

The enemy is a fallen angel, a created being. He had served in the Temple of God as a worshipping angel, second in command in heaven under God, and had great authority given to him by God. He arrogantly chose to declare himself to be equal with God, and this caused his fall and disgrace for all time and eternity.

Jesus is the Son of God. He is not a created being. He is God manifested in human form, so we could be ransomed from the law of sin and death through His sacrifice. The perfect, spotless Lamb of God is also the Lion of Judah, who devoured our enemies and conquered sin, death and the grave.

Jesus has no equal. He has been given all power and authority over everything in the heavens and on earth. Before Him, every knee shall bow, and every tongue confess that He, alone, is Lord over all!

This changed everything.

CHAPTER 19:

BRILLIANCE IN BATTLE

As I've shared this with folks over the years, some say I focus too much on the enemy. I've been admonished not to talk so much about him. It might scare people!

It seems to me we aren't winning many battles with this strategy of ignoring the enemy and denying his tactics. It makes me wonder if staying ignorant of the enemy's devices isn't a clever ploy of the enemy himself.

In my studies, I've come to believe all military strategists would agree it's important to know your enemy before you meet him on the battlefield.

Is it possible that like me, many have made Jesus so small, so powerless and rather wimpy, we have to keep our image of the enemy even smaller just to maintain some kind of hope?

In this battle I was walking through, as the enemy tried to power up on me and present himself as the stronger one, Jesus not only rose up to face the enemy head-on over me but He was out in front of the enemy heading him off, exposing his plans and utterly defeating him.

Jesus was brilliance in action.

The intellect of the enemy, with all his evil, cunning savvy, is no match for the wisdom and power of the Most High God! There wasn't anything the enemy could throw at Him that He was not able to easily overcome. Nothing took Him by surprise. There was never a time when Jesus was anything but confident, on the move, pushing the enemy back as He reminded him of the finished work of the Cross.

Jesus is perfect love and perfect valiant warrior at the same time. He is kind, tender, merciful, and full of grace as much as He is full of strength, valor, judgment, and justice.

I had known Him one way. He was revealing Himself another. Not instead of, but in addition to. I was seeing Jesus more completely.

He was my refuge, my place to hide myself in. He was also my defender, my protector, the keeper of my soul. As ruthless as the enemy was in the ways of cruelty and wickedness, Jesus was fierce in battle in victorious love with divine justice.

I was in awe of my Lord and King.

As the heavens began to close, and quiet came back to the room, the angel said to me, "There is none His equal."

There's only one response in His presence, and that was to worship Him. Everything within me delighted to give Him the glory, the honor, and the adoration He deserved.

True to Pastor Wayne's word, this was an intense time of training for me. My eyes were being opened. These were life-changing lessons about these two kingdoms engaged in this age-old conflict over the eternal souls of every man, woman, and child ever born.

CHAPTER 20:

DEVIL'S PLAYBOOK

The system operations of the kingdom of darkness were being exposed. Patterns were revealed as the enemy was being routed. Basically, it looked like this:

First, the enemy and his cohorts would orchestrate some kind of harm. They would use the evil resources they had in men and women who had either yielded to him or who had deep wounds of their own that had never been healed by the blood of Jesus.

It didn't matter to them how this came about necessarily but the greater the harm, the deeper the wound. The deeper the wound, the greater the pain. The greater the pain, the greater advantage the enemy gained to do more long-term harm.

This is why the enemy always aimed to cut deep, jagged, dirty wounds. Sexual abuse is a favorite tool of his to use against both men and women, the younger, the better.

Once the initial harm happened, he began filling the innocent victim's mind with all kinds of lies. The enemy wants to get this individual into a place of bitterness quickly. It's the first wall built to keep the victim isolated. To accomplish this, one tactic he uses is blaming everyone and everything while keeping the victims' eyes off the enemy as the real source of the wound.

The enemy is adept at pointing the finger at people or circumstances to cover his evil work. He whispers whatever lies necessary to get the person to buy into his agenda.

Once the lie is received, an open door is created. He keeps hammering at the wound and re-enforces the lie. It effectively isolates the victim from help, and they come to believe that their situation is hopeless; that they are unworthy of freedom, and are unlovable.

Have you ever noticed how one sexual abuse leads to another?

This is a strategy of the enemy, adding hurt upon hurt to enforce his lies and strengthen the walls. The ways he does this is varied.

As I mentioned earlier, he can use other people who have been wounded as his puppets to speak and/or do horrible things. The schemes are planned to bring the greatest harm in the deepest way possible to as many as possible.

Layer upon layer, a tight grip is formed around the wounded heart, choking the life out of them. Of course, if he sees an opportunity, he will add to the wounds, wrapping chain upon chain to strengthen his hold.

If the person tries to get help from the world's system, the enemy will usually shove them into it. He knows better than we do how ineffective the world is against him. If an individual seeks their freedom from the world, they end up in worse shape and with more open doors. In fact, the enemy himself will actually lead the wounded to all kinds of false healers, where they pick up more wounding.

But if the person tries to get help from God's people, the enemy will double up on them. He will try to bury them under shame, guilt, accusation, and condemnation, until they feel unworthy of being free, and fall back in despair.

Once the individual accepts the lies and gives up in defeat, they pick up the enemy's work against themselves. They become their own accuser.

This all culminates in the person wounding themselves for the rest of their lives, and is the leading cause of suicide. The enemy merely stands back and laughs.

The victim is now a plaything in the enemy's hand. His work is almost effortless.

Remember, the enemy never fights fair. There's nothing good in him. Nothing!

Also, it's critical for us as adults to never forget his favorite targets are children. If he can start this cycle at a young age, it is more difficult to take back the lost ground, but it is not impossible. With God, all things are possible!

This is what I was now doing in my life. Taking back what the enemy had stolen.

To do that required mentally and emotionally re-visiting painful places; the very event where those wounds first occurred. To do less meant we were merely putting cotton balls on the bleeding artery. We wanted to fix the root of the problem, to take back the ground. This was essential to close the doors and remove the enemy's ability to come and go at his whim.

We had been praying our way through this very work for three days now. All of us were tired. It had been rough, and I couldn't imagine there was anything more to be done. My heart felt light. I was excited about this new place of freedom that had been gained. It was a good place to go on living from. I was willing to call it good and be thankful for the freedom I had gained.

Pastor Wayne and Deanna prayed about it and felt there were a couple of things we needed to address first. I trusted their wisdom even if I didn't see the need. We had already talked about the big bad stuff, so I felt confident this was clean-up mode, like picking up the stragglers. I took it rather lightly.

On my questionnaire, I had shared with Pastor Wayne my innate fear of water. Specifically, being underwater. To me, it wasn't a big deal. People had all kinds of phobias, such as the fear of the dark, or fear of heights. The fear of water happened to be mine. I had learned how to manage it, and it wasn't debilitating to my life.

He asked me to explain it a bit more.

If I had any sensation remotely resembling being suffocated, I would panic and freak out! A paralyzing fear would grip hold of me, and I was literally unable to move my limbs. My remedy was to avoid getting myself into deep water where there was a risk of drowning if the panic took hold.

Again, I didn't think this was anything noteworthy. It seemed pretty common to me.

He asked me to explain if there were any other times I would feel this fear of water.

Yes, I continued rather embarrassed. I couldn't put my face in the water while showering. If water ran down my face, that same unreasonable fear would consume me. I felt foolish for saying this. Nobody drowns in their shower!

"Anything else?" he asked.

Well, I couldn't pass swim lessons as a kid. I could kick, have my strokes down, and float with the best of them, but absolutely would not put my face in the water. I flunked the swimming test every time, because it involved jumping off the edge in the deep end, which resulted in an underwater plunge, before swimming to the shallow end. Oh, and forget diving. That's not happening.

Pastor Wayne listened and then began to pray. He asked Holy Spirit to bring to mind where this fear came from.

We sat quietly, waiting.

I told him I got nothing. I'm thinking to myself this isn't really a big deal. We can move on.

After a time, Deanna came behind me, laid her hands on my shoulders, and started humming the hymn, "It is Well with My Soul."

The song itself was written by a man who lost all of his children when their ship went down at sea, his wife survived. He and his wife returned to the spot where the ship sank, and God gave him this song. There are a lot of references to water in it.

Deanna has a beautiful voice. Her voice had always been comforting to me. Not this time!

As she hummed, it was like fingernails on the chalkboard. An agitation started deep within me and began to bubble to the surface. I wanted to scream at her to stop. Then I wanted to make her stop. I had no idea where this was coming from. The strong emotions were alarming to me, and I didn't understand what was happening.

All I knew was, it wasn't well with my soul!

Absolute terror filled my heart as the memory slowly surfaced from deep within my mind. At the same time, I felt the angels around me lift their chests as they geared up for battle.

This was going to be bad. Very bad.

CHAPTER 21:

BABYSITTER WITH A HATCHET

As I previously mentioned, when they took my daddy to the hospital, he was placed on life support. He was an organ donor, and they were preparing the recipients of his body parts. The entire process took five days; I was told years later.

I was taken to the baby-sitter's house. The house where the man lived.

After my mother dropped me off, the man went into the living room and sat down in his recliner. I don't know where the wife went. The man called me to him. When I went over, he lifted me onto his lap.

I was very worried about my daddy, not knowing what was happening to him. I didn't know where my three sisters were. I wanted my mom to stay with me. I wanted to be with the rest of my family, but I was here. Six years old. Alone. In this strange man's lap. Expecting to be comforted, I snuggled in.

What greeted me instead was this man using my body for his perverse pleasure. I was fully clothed, but him grinding against me hurt.

This was all wrong. A terrible fear settled on my heart.

On the following days, this man took me into his bedroom. The lights were off, and the shades were drawn. He said we were going to take a nap together. Each day he was more aggressive with his touching.

On this day, he started taking my clothes off. Fear paralyzed me. Standing in just my panties, he told me to get under the covers and stay there.

I crawled into the bed and pulled the covers under my chin. He came over to me and pulled the covers over my head. I was completely covered. I didn't like this and uncovered my head. He told me if dared to poke as much as my foot out, he would chop it off. He lifted up a hatchet that was on the nightstand. I believed him. He covered my head again.

He undressed, got under the covers with me, and tried to force me to perform sexual acts on him. I was horrified! I began to fight him, which made him very angry.

He got up, telling me to stay under the covers, or else! He went into the bathroom. I could hear what sounded like water in the bathtub. He came back, grabbed me, and drug me into the bathroom, dropping me into the bathtub.

Next thing I knew, he was holding my head under the water. I was terrified and fought hard. He would pull my head up by my hair, and I gasped for air. I don't know how many times this was done, but it didn't end until I had no strength to fight.

He pulled me up to within inches of my face and told me if I ever fought him again, people I loved would die. He would make sure of it! I immediately thought about my sick daddy, afraid for his life.

He took me back under the covers. Again, he forced me to participate in oral sex. This time, I didn't fight.

The next day, my mom came by to tell us my daddy had died.

I learned in later years that this man already knew my daddy was legally dead because he had been on life support for five days before he died. He knew, but I didn't know. He used that knowledge to utterly crush my spirit and manipulate my young mind.

My mom was asking the wife if she could keep me at their house for a few days while she planned the funeral. I begged to be taken with her to no avail.

She left me at the man's house.

As I sat in this room with Pastor Wayne and Deanna, the safest place I had known in my young life, I suddenly knew the source of my nightmares.

They weren't childish concoctions from an evil heart as I had always thought. I had believed the lies the enemy had whispered to me. No, these nightmares were born from the deep, agonizing, unattended pain of sexual perversion and abuse washing over me as I slept. The nightmares were based on true events my young mind was trying to reckon but unable to process.

I sat in this place, in this moment, as a great agony of heart overwhelmed me. Suddenly, an evil laughter filled the room. It was a guttural sound dripping with the slimy stench of lust. The enemy began taunting and mocking me:

You know you wanted it.

You are nasty and dirty and damaged.

You liked what he did to you, why did you fight him?

If you fight us, your daddy will die! Oh wait, he did die!

They laughed and mocked my pain.

I remembered my paternal grandmother telling me I was to blame for my daddy's death. Another deep pain stabbed like a knife to my heart.

I remember my maternal grandmother calling me a liar when I was attacked by a man attempting to molest me. She betrayed me in front of the police who knew this man had many other charges of child molestation against him while she refused to be a part of the solution. I saw myself in the car on the long drive home with my mother. Silence was our companion. She would not look at me, would not speak to me, and also accused me of lying. This accusation she has carried against me my entire life, to this very day.

Heaving sobs escaped my throat. I felt the suffocating fear of being held underwater, fighting to breathe, the darkness closing in. I felt the familiar panic overtaking me. I wanted to run and hide. I was desperate to escape. I needed to get free.

Then, I started seeing the faces of other men. This time, I was watching from a distance as these men were using my young body in various forms or fashion: different men, different times in different ways. I saw their faces, and heard their cruel, lurid laughter.

I also saw the stark terror on my round childish face. It was like a demonized feeding frenzy, feasting on my hurt and pain. The more scared I was, the greater their evil delight.

As I was looking down on these scenes from the past, I beheld this small little girl, devastated over the death of her daddy, being abused by evil men for their personal depravity; abandoned, rejected and betrayed by those who should have kept her safe, and an intense grief swept over me like a physical ache.

There were no words to speak. All I had to express the agony I was feeling were deep groanings of gut-wrenching pain.

I was grieving the loss of her innocence.

I mourned the loss of her carefree childhood.

I was broken by the deep wounds inflicted on her tiny heart.

It was easier to grieve from a distance. Finally, I had to accept the fact that the "her" I cried for was, in fact me.

In this room, not knowing how I got there, I was on the floor huddled in a fetal position. I was sick to my stomach. I cried ragged, ugly sobs until there were no more tears to cry. For a long time. An incredible sense of shame swept over me like a physical ache.

Far off, I heard Pastor Wayne and Deanna praying over me. Their prayers were grounding me, pulling me back to the safe place I needed to be to face what was tormenting me.

As I lay there utterly exhausted and spent, I looked over at Pastor Wayne. Both he and Deanna were sitting on the floor with me. Deanna was beside me, quietly praying. I saw tears running down her face.

With swollen eyes and a scratchy voice, I told Pastor Wayne, "If you tell me I have to repent for this, I may hurt you."

I wasn't kidding. I meant it. What on earth did I have to repent for?

I could see in His eyes immeasurable compassion and fierce determination. He firmly but gently asked, "What do you feel towards your mother for leaving you there?"

Resentment. Why did she leave me there? Where were my sisters? Why didn't she know this man was evil? As I remembered my fear as a child, a deep bitterness towards her rose to the surface.

I loved my mother, as children do, but I didn't trust her. I couldn't remember a time when I had. I didn't feel safe with her. I wanted to be loved by her, accepted and close, but I felt betrayed by her. Abandoned. Rejected. Discarded. Alone.

Pastor Wayne then asked me, "What do you feel towards these men and what they did to you?"

Instantly, I spat out the word. Hate. I hate them. All of them. I want them to suffer for what they did and die painfully. I want them all to go to hell!

The tears started flowing again. I felt ashamed for feeling that way. Hate didn't seem right, but the hate in me had gone deep. It never had a voice before, but it was there.

Pastor Wayne's penetrating eyes looked right into me as he said, "That is what you need to repent of. Those feelings of resentment, bitterness, hate, guilt, and shame are keeping you bound to this pain. This is a wide-open door. You will not gain freedom until you repent of these feelings."

I wish I could say those prayers flowed out of me graciously. They didn't.

I agonized over them.

There was nothing in me that wanted to repent for my feelings. I felt justified in them. They had been my companions for a long time even though buried deep. They were the cement in the walls I had built to keep my heart safe. Nobody else kept me safe, so I learned to build great walls. They were a sick form of comfort to me.

When I looked up, I saw there was a battle being fought all around me. The enemy was strong. I had nurtured them well for many years. He was relentless in his fight to keep me in bondage.

The angels were standing their ground but had taken some very hard hits. They were largely outnumbered in this battle.

I saw the one angel I was looking for. He was standing between me and several very large enemies who were fixated on bringing me harm. From the fierce warrior look on his face, I knew he would not leave this place of protection over me willingly. He would suffer loss and even death to see me kept safe.

As we locked eyes, he was speaking to me without words, imparting courage to take my stand and break free. Beyond my natural understanding, I knew deep in the core of my being that this battle would only end when I humbled my heart and repented.

With that understanding, something deep within me broke.

I began to pray.

It didn't come from my feelings or natural desire. It was a complete act of my will. I had to set my mind to obey God regardless of my emotions raging within me.

Once I opened my mouth and started speaking, Holy Spirit came in power.

The next thing I knew, I was standing on my feet with His courage burning deep within. Holy Spirit was pouring over me like warm oil. My voice grew stronger, and I was speaking loudly, adamantly, no longer cowering in the fetal position on the floor.

I repented until there was nothing more to say.

Then I took the authority I have as a child of the Most High God through the precious Blood of Jesus. As I began to pray, a surge of new strength came over the angels.

I bound these enemies with chains and fetters of iron and cast them away from me. I submitted my heart to God, resisted the enemy and declared loudly, "Be gone!"

The angels quickly routed the enemy, banishing them from this place, from my life. They were battered, their shields bearing the marks of war, yet they were smiling the smiles of conquerors after a hard-won victory and a battle well fought.

The room grew quiet with the presence of Holy Spirit.

We all joined in prayer as Pastor Wayne asked Holy Spirit to hold me close and fill me with His Truth, His comfort, and His power. I felt surrounded in perfect peace. Holy Spirit held me in His arms as these angelic warriors stood watch. I was utterly spent, and my heart felt raw, but free.

It had been four long days of fighting for my freedom. The freedom Jesus died to restore to each of us by shedding His precious Blood. All of us were exhausted, yet light of heart.

I was crying grateful tears, sweet tears that poured down my face. My heart was filled with thanksgiving.

Before I left for home, Pastor Wayne prayed over us all. He was diligent in setting up a hedge of protection around me, asking Holy Spirit to guard my heart and keep my mind.

We parted with plans to meet the next morning. It was time to finish this battle.

CHAPTER 22:

SHINY BLACK FLOOR

As we met the next morning, I once again felt confident all was well. I had prayed and asked God to show me if there was anything else, and nothing came to mind. It had been grueling, and we all were tired.

Once we all sat down, I shared this with Pastor Wayne. He smiled and seemed glad to hear it.

He again opened our time in prayer, asking Holy Spirit to lead us in His power. Then he looked at me as said he wanted me to close my eyes and rest in the presence of God. He was going to repeat a phrase to me in a language I would not know. However, Holy Spirit would tell me the meaning of the phrase. I just needed to listen.

I learned later, that this was how he tested the spirits to make sure the work was complete. Pastor Wayne believed in praying through until Holy Spirit said it was done.

So, I closed my eyes, intent on listening. I had no doubt Holy Spirit would tell me the meaning of the phrase, and I waited to hear.

Nothing. There was silence. I continued to wait, but no answer came.

Pastor Wayne didn't seem surprised by this, but I was. I so wanted this to be over and done with. He and Deanna began to pray and ask Holy Spirit to show me my heart.

As they prayed, I saw a large cavern. It had stalactites and stalagmites, and was beautifully illuminated by a warm glow. The walls were covered in beautiful crystal formations. It was a welcoming place.

I walked around, looking behind every rock, into crevices and alcoves to see if something was hiding. There was nothing.

Pastor Wayne and Deanna continued to pray. As they did, I sat down on a rock. I was also praying, asking for wisdom to see what I needed to see.

As I sat there, I looked down at the floor. It was beautiful. It looked like black onyx, gleaming in the soft glow of light. It had a mirror finish; it was so shiny.

Suddenly, out of the corner of my eye, I saw what looked like the floor moving. I was looking intently now, and sure enough, it wiggled slightly. I pulled my feet up onto the rock and shared with Pastor Wayne what I was seeing.

He began to pray and call out the enemy hiding in this manner. As he did, out of the floor rose a hideous creature like I had never seen before. It was black, tarry, and smelled horrible. A mixture of sulphur and dead animals is how I would describe the smell. It was awful.

As this creature revealed more of itself, I saw it had long talons that were oozing a tar- like substance. Its eyes were like red laser beams boring into me. This being had fangs dripping with blood, and smoke was pouring out of its nostrils with every exhale. It looked like a demonic dragon, living in an oozy tar pit.

I was sharing this with Pastor Wayne, and I remember him saying, "I see it. It's okay." He began praying against this evil creature who called itself Deception.

It began boasting of all the torture it had inflicted upon my life through its craftiness. It called me stupid along with other unflattering epitaphs. It was arrogant and proud of its destruction, unwavering in its desire to kill my children and me.

This demonic being mocked me for my weakness in calling out for help. It mocked the other demonic entities that had been cast out of my life as weaklings, deserving of the abyss, but not him! He would never leave. He was the one who came into my life first, and he was staying, he declared. His voice was loud and snarly.

He described how he brought the evil men into my life. He was so proud as he told me the things he still had planned for my life, to destroy me. He laughed at his own words.

Deceptions' stated purpose was to keep me from the Truth of God's Word. Through hurt followed by false teachers spewing false teaching, he kept me from knowing who I was in Christ.

This evil being had stolen my identity.

He had brought his henchman, through other wounded people, into my life. They led me to believe things about myself that opposed what God said about me.

As it spoke, it seemed to grow in size until it filled the entire cave. It enveloped me with its evil darkness, and I felt the fear, the panic, and the hopelessness I had lived with most of my life. He was attempting to pull me into the inky tar with him.

But I wasn't the same little lost girl I had been all those years. I now knew who I was in the Kingdom of God as a blood-bought child of the King of Kings!

I could hear Pastor Wayne and Deanna praying over me, I could see the angels taking their stance to prepare for this battle, and I knew the authority I had to defeat this foe. Regardless of how large and foreboding he was, I believed Jesus was greater.

I realized I had chosen to believe the lies of deception, follow false teaching, and esteem men over the Truth found in God's Word. I saw clearly how I had fed this demonic giant since I was six years old; possibly earlier in my childhood. I saw his tentacles wrapped around my heart, and could feel them trying to squeeze the very life out of me.

Pastor Wayne had taught me well over these past months. I began to repent for accepting the lying words of deception.

Chunk. I felt a tentacle fall off of me.

I repented for believing what this evil creature had said to me about myself and about others rather than what God said.

Clunk. Another tentacle broke off.

I repented for falsely accusing my King and Lord by calling His Word a lie, when it was the Truth that set me free.

Clunk, clunk. This evil being was being sliced into pieces as the warring angels fought with their Swords of Truth, my prayers enforcing their strength.

This battle didn't last long, even though this demonic entity was the kingpin. It was the foundation on which every other evil in my life had been laid.

He was the first to come and the last to go!

When this creature was forced to flee in the wonderful Name of Jesus, we all began to pray. We asked for my heart to be filled with the presence of the Most High God through the indwelling of His Holy Spirit. We consecrated it to Him for His eternal purposes as I knelt before Him in humility and gratefulness for His faithfulness.

When I looked back at this cave, the floor was no longer black. It shone like diamonds. The light danced across it, shimmering with colors that seemed to be alive with joy. The same songs I heard in the rivers as a child were echoing in this place, resounding off the walls and filling me to full and overflowing with joy.

When I looked into Pastor Wayne and Deanna's face, I saw peace. We all sat back in our chairs, cherishing this moment.

Once again, Pastor Wayne said the phrase in a language I did not know. This time, I knew what it meant. Beyond any doubt, I knew the words.

I spoke it out loud, and he smiled – his own face reflecting the joy overwhelming me.

The enemy had been routed out of my heart and my life by the precious and holy Name of Jesus. It was because of His shed blood that I was now free.

Praise the Holy and Precious Name of Jesus Christ, our Savior, Redeemer, and Lord!

This battle was over.

CHAPTER 23:

VICTORY

After a peaceful night's sleep, I woke up feeling like I had been in the ring with a professional boxer. My body ached in places that I didn't know existed.

However, my spirit was refreshed, restored, and soaring. I tested my heart and found it to be light and filled with a deep joy I knew wasn't of this world.

I took a drive out to a local lake and went for a long walk along its edge. I was thinking and pondering about what had transpired over the past five days. It felt surreal. Otherworldly. Supernatural.

I couldn't deny what I had experienced. There was no explaining away what Pastor Wayne, Deanna, and I had witnessed and walked through together.

I had so many questions.

As agreed, I returned in the early afternoon to connect with Pastor Wayne and Deanna. We hugged and greeted one another like soldiers returning from battle. It was the camaraderie of fellow warriors forged by the battles we had shared. I had learned how real this analogy was.

Wisely, they knew all things of lasting value must be built on the Biblical foundation of the Word of God with Jesus Christ as the Corner Stone. If not, it would not stand. They wasted no time continuing to build my faith.

As we gathered, I looked at them and simply asked, "What just happened?"

"As one of God's children," Pastor Wayne explained, "you are a critical part of an age-old spiritual war between the kingdom of darkness and God's Kingdom of Light."

How true this is for each of us. We are born onto a battlefield. Once we find salvation in Jesus, we are able to engage the enemy as more than conquerors, no longer defeated victims.

The battle we had just come through was real. As it replayed in my mind, nobody had to tell me the war was intense, and the enemy played for keeps, with his only goal my eternal destruction.

When I recounted the many ways the enemy had nearly accomplished his evil end in my own life, I couldn't help feeling overwhelmed with thanksgiving. I also grieved, because I knew there were so many people I loved and cared about who were still captive behind enemy lines.

As I came through this battle, I saw the size of the enemies that had fallen. I heard their carefully woven schemes, far above my intelligence. As I recalled the pure evil we had faced, a tremor of fear ran through me.

Then I thought about Pastor Wayne and Deanna and their fearless confidence when facing off with the host of hell. I remembered time and time again when Pastor Wayne drove back the powers of darkness, and how they quaked and fled when he stood against them.

Several Bible stories came to mind. David meeting Goliath with bold confidence. Daniel in the lions' den with no fear. Shadrach, Meshach, and Abednego facing the fiery furnace with faith. So many examples of courage in the face of overpowering darkness.

Obviously, they all knew things I still needed to learn.

I didn't know how to get there, but I knew I wanted this same courage!

"As in any war," Pastor Wayne continued, "there are weapons at our disposal. Our Lord and Savior did not leave us ill-equipped or unprepared for this battle. He gave us many tools to use that are effective in walking as overcomers in His Name. Because we are grafted into His Kingdom through the Blood of Jesus, we have been given the same authority Jesus had to overcome every wicked device of the enemy. We need to have our hands trained for war and become equipped to stand."

I was sitting on the edge of my seat in rapt attention, eager to know more.

Little did I know; the enemy was prowling close.

CHAPTER 24:

I'LL BE BACK

Somewhere within me, I wanted to believe the erroneous lie that once the enemy had been driven from my life, he wouldn't bother coming back. I made the grave error of applying basic human decency to the realm of darkness.

My reasoning required him to show mercy and give me time to rest. After all, he lost the battle fair and square. I needed to be refreshed and enjoy this new place, unencumbered by his nastiness. Surely, he would leave me alone.

Obviously, I had more growing up to do. For starters, I needed to stop being naïve.

Pastor Wayne continued to mentor me. "Once he is driven out, and the doors to your life have been closed through repentance, he has to leave," Pastor Wayne explained. "But being true to his evil nature, it's only a temporary loss to him, because as long as there is breath in you, the war is not over for him."

He went on to explain how the enemy circles, stalks, and slinks around, watching for any open door where he can strike. One of his favorite tools is to use the same scheme he used in our past; launching again the fiery dart that had worked before.

This is an effective scheme, because it catches you off guard and causes confusion when it hits. He'll whisper in your ear that you were never set free. He will taunt and torment you with past thoughts and feelings, while trying to bury you under shame and guilt.

This is a crucial point of decision. To believe his lie is to invite him back in to set up camp in your life!

I was beginning to learn how crucial the armor of God is, especially the helmet of salvation. I needed to renew my mind to believe the Word of God above any voice.

It was critical for me to walk in the understanding that anything not aligning with God's Word is not to be accepted as Truth, regardless of who is speaking. This bears repeating over and over, until it is grafted into us as a part of our core being.

A-N-Y-T-H-I-N-G that does not align with God's Word is not to be accepted as Truth, regardless of who is speaking.

I heard the words, and I sincerely believed them, but they had not yet been grafted into my spirit as a part of my core being. I was unskilled in using my weapons of war.

Not far out of the starting gate, the enemy hit hard. I fell hard. But God was holding my hand, as He promises He will, so I did not fall headlong.

This is what happened.

CHAPTER 25:

LOVE STORY

As I've shared with you, I had spent the majority of my days feeling unworthy of love, damaged and unlovable. The enemy invested into the greater portion of my life, hammering this lie into me until it became my false identity.

He spent years re-enforcing the lie with circumstances, comments from other people and assaulting my mind even as I slept. The lie had gone deep.

Then I met Jesus personally. Not only did He save me, but He also rescued me from the lies. I came to believe that I was a beloved child of the King of Kings and Lord of Lords.

This newly found freedom was a joy to me. One that I cherished and valued as a rich treasure.

For a brief time, the enemy was not able to torment me. However, his temporary loss did not stop him from his relentless pursuit to take me captive once again. He couldn't wait to get me back behind enemy lines.

In our society that values quick and effortless, we must embrace the Truth that freedom is not a one and done proposition. There is a battle to get free and a battle to stay free.

Quickly, the enemy began chipping away at my freedom by using the same accusations from my past. At first, I recognized them and stood strong against them. However, he kept whispering his convincing lies against my value and worth at every opportunity. He would use family to remind me of my many failures since childhood. Strangely, the evil words felt familiar, comfortable in a perverted and twisted way.

Bit by bit, the old feelings of inadequacy and being unlovable started to overwhelm me. These thoughts weren't coming from within me, but were like smoke drifting around me, polluting the air I was breathing and clouding my ability to see clearly.

In a short time, I no longer recognized the lies for what they were. I had not yet spent enough time renewing my mind with the Truth from God's Word about who I am in Him.
Soon, I was struggling with believing God could love me.

The tactic was sly because it didn't doubt God's ability to love me; it doubted my worthiness of His love. This fed into a very old wound in me that had been healed, but was still very tender. The accusations were like picking a scab off and exposing raw flesh that hadn't quite healed.

The attack came in under my radar. Before long, I had been lulled into an evil, weird spiritual sleep.

However, I wasn't standing alone any longer. There were at least two wonderful people committed to praying over me each day. On top of that, I had a host of angels standing guard over me, and the Holy Spirit of God Himself lived within me.

An alarm was sounded in my spirit that could not be ignored. It shook me out of the slumber.

As I jolted out of the spiritual stupor I was being lulled into, I was terrified looking around me. I had come dangerously close to fully opening the door once again to the enemy.

As it was, I could see the door bulging inwardly with his lies, like battering rams, trying to knock down the barrier between us. I knew in the depths of my being that he was lurking on the other side, crying out in vengeance against my escape. He was out for my blood.

The next thing I knew, I was lying on my face on the floor before God.

I repented for entertaining those evil thoughts and cried out for His help. I began clumsily praying on the armor of God, specifically clothing my mind with the Helmet of Salvation. I remembered my authority and commanded the enemy to leave me alone. In a short time, peace was restored, but it left me shaken.

As I lay in this place, I asked God to show me how to stop the enemy from tormenting me this way. I wanted to see my life through the eyes of God. I desperately wanted to see what He saw in me.

As I laid on the floor in the presence of His peace, this is what I saw.

The angel I had come to know during those five days of battle was standing in front of me. He held out His hand, and our eyes met. He was beckoning me to trust him, and I took his hand. As I did, we were immediately soaring through the heavens.

We arrived back at the beginning, before there was time.

As I looked down, we were hovering over dark roiling waters. The only light was coming off of the angel beside me. The angry black waters extended beyond what the light revealed. There was no sun, moon or stars - nothing but inky darkness and raging black seas.

Then we were ascending. As we did, I looked up. There was a host of angels filling a beautiful place. There was light from a source I didn't know. The angels extended far beyond what I could see. When I looked closely at them, they were fixed intently on something out of my vision. There was an air of anticipation and uncertainty, like something was about to happen, but none of them knew what it was.

The angel and I were in this beautiful place, looking down over the waters when suddenly, a loud commanding Voice thundered through all the empty space. I can't remember understanding the words themselves, but felt them deep within me.

I did not see the source of the Voice, but somehow, I knew He knew me well. Without being told, I knew in my heart of hearts that this was the Voice of my Heavenly Father.

As He spoke, cataclysmic events began happening in rapid succession. His Voice alone was bringing to life substance where once there was nothing.

He formed the sun for warmth, the moon to light our way at night and the stars that glimmer and shine as signs in what is now called heaven. He fashioned the air we breathe, water from all manner of bubbly flowing sources, the lush soft grass beneath our feet, and every kind of plant for our nourishment and healing. He fashioned many kinds of animals, birds of the air, and fish of the sea.

All around, life was being created. Simply because He spoke.

Creation was filled with vibrancy, color, and songs I had never experienced before. Each flower petal was intricately designed with beauty beyond anything I had seen. They moved and fluttered in the wind, singing songs of praise and worship to their Creator. Their scent was beyond imagination, and each breath was life-giving, invigorating.

I heard songs in the waters as they rolled over the stones. Each roll of the tiny waves was singing different songs, yet all in perfect harmony one with another. It was stunning and glorious, and no words could ever describe this place.

I looked up and saw as the angels watched in wonder and awe at all He was doing. They were curiously enthralled at the passion with which He worked. Their excitement was building as they shared in the unfolding of this incredible secret that had been hidden from them. This was being birthed before us all from the very heart of God.

It was apparent to all of us observers these were not random acts. This work was intentional by design, building day upon day. All of heaven held its breath as this amazing creation materialized out of thin air before us.

We were in awe! The atmosphere was energized with tremendous love and delight flowing from Heavenly Father's presence. There was dancing, worship and a time of great celebration as each new discovery unfolded.

The angel turned to me and said with the most loving smile on his face, "The unfolding of creation is far more than the story of how the world came to be. It's so much richer, sweeter, and far deeper. The story of creation is the sweetest love story of all time!"

I looked back with fresh eyes at everything that was being formed right before me. Slowly, the Truth of his words began to settle deep into my spirit.

Creation was the work of a Lover preparing the perfect trysting place for His cherished one.

When everything was put in perfect order, Heavenly Father gave birth to the ultimate desire of His heart. He created for Himself a companion; a reflection of His image. A being He could have an intimate and personal relationship with.

He created Adam; the cherished and adored apple of His eye.

Instantly, I saw Heavenly Father's great delight when this very special work was done!

Oh, how He enjoyed walking with Adam in the garden. They communed together while naming the animals. They listened to the birds, heard songs of joy in the rivers, and watched the fish playing in the many waters.

Being with Adam brought Heavenly Father extreme joy and pleasure.

Then something amazing took place. Birthed from the character of His own nature and His desire for intimacy, Heavenly Father knew it was not good for Adam to be alone. He knew this before Adam did, because He had created Adam with the need for intimacy.

In His tender loving care over His beloved son, He created a perfect counterpart who would walk with Adam. Adam named her Eve.

Of all living creatures, there were none who were created in the same way as Eve. Eve's beginning was not taken from the dirt of the earth, nor was she spoken into existence. Eve was formed from a physical piece of Adam.

God caused a deep sleep to fall upon Adam, and He actually removed one of his ribs. From that rib, He formed Eve and breathed life into her as He did Adam. Eve was an extension of Adam himself.

Adam cherished her, desired to be with her, and extended to her all that he was. Adam knew how to love Eve because He had first experienced it from His Heavenly Father who taught him while they walked in the garden together.
Eve delighted in Adam, walked by his side, and enjoyed his company with pure abandonment as they both experienced a deeply intimate relationship with God, their Father.

Adam and Eve ran through the fields, swam in the oceans, and played in the meadows as they lovingly took dominion over the garden as they had been commanded by God. All the while, they explored the wonder and delights of each other. Their love was the expression of God's hearts' desire for His creation.

Considerable time of great length passed as we all relished in this amazing event.

Truly, this was paradise!

CHAPTER 26:

AGONY IN HEAVEN

Suddenly, it all changed. We were celebrating this amazing creation when an agonizing cry tore through the heavenlies. This was a cry of sorrow that wailed and rolled upon the winds with a violent force.

We had to cover our ears, but nothing blocked out the sound. It was deafening, and was felt in the depths of our being.

The hair on the back of my neck stood up as I was driven to my knees. An evil fear began to encroach upon this peaceful paradise. Something was terribly wrong.

Time seemed to stand still as the echoes of agony reached beyond the galaxies and swept back over us. The angels bowed low and covered their faces at the sound of mourning.

I buried my head in my hands, sobbing uncontrollably, unable to bear the depths of this unfettered grief. In that instant, I knew if these gut-wrenching cries did not stop, I would surely die under the crushing weight of this unexplained agony.

Then, the ground shuddered. Another cry reached my ears. It was the eerie sound of creation groaning as it shuddered.

The ground shook violently, and the force of it split it in two. A deep gash in the earth formed. Waters dried up, beauty faded, colors were muted, and the songs were silent. The sweet aroma was fouled with a tar-like scent, and the animals who had existed in peace were now filled with rage.

What did it all mean?

After much time, the dust and smoke settled. There was a collective gasp in the heavenlies as the meaning of these catastrophic events started to appear. Understanding began to dawn, and sorrow upon sorrow continued to roll through the heavens, descending to earth.

Sin had entered the garden.

This was the most grievous day ever in the history of the world. My stomach was sick, and my heart physically hurt as I looked upon the scene far below.

I watched this evil change creep over the garden like a thick black fog.

My perception of what this day held had always been limited to how it affected mankind.   I was familiar with what we had lost through that willful decision to sin by disobeying God. I knew that wickedness was given place in the earth, and evil came to reside within the heart of man. I've always been heartsick at all that was forfeited, and rightfully so.

But seeing this play out before me, I realized I had never stopped and thought about what Heavenly Father had lost on that fateful day. Sin changed everything for our Holy and Righteous God.

No longer could He walk with Adam in the dew of the morning, or take Eve by the hand and run through the wildflowers. The sweet times of listening to them prattle on about their new discoveries, of watching their wonder as they strolled through the garden had been stolen.

The choice to sin severed relationship and intimacy with our Heavenly Father.

Hot tears rolled down my face. Finally, I dared to open my eyes and look once again.

There, I saw Adam and Eve. They didn't look the same. I had to look closely before I realized what was different.

When intimacy with God was severed by sin, the immediate result was the loss of intimacy with one another. Adam and Eve saw each other differently. Their love was marred. They were arguing.

Dissension came as they blamed one another before God. They now viewed one another through lenses tainted with suspicion, judgment, and betrayal. Purity was clouded with murky darkness.

Strife replaced the unity they had once shared. The sweetness of their love was replaced with self-gratifying thoughts of entitlement. Sexual intimacy was shifted into carnal lust.

What was once given freely to each other now became an expected duty to multiply. Offenses took root, resentment gained a place, and a root of bitterness was established. This root would affect countless generations, causing many to be defiled.

What had been so very sweetly right in their relationship was now all very wrong. When sin had entered the garden, shame entered into their hearts.

Shame is always the legacy sin leaves behind.

I watched as God, filled with a terrible sadness, killed the very animals He had created for their enjoyment. The shedding of innocent blood was the price paid to cover Adam and Eve's sin. Sin now sullied their oneness with God and their oneness with each other.

Heaven was rent in two, battle lines were drawn, angels fell, and Adam and Eve had to leave the Garden.

Never again would they share in the sweet intimacy with God they had been created for. The choice to sin had changed it all.

All of heaven wept.

Heavenly Father's heart grieved with agony far beyond my ability with mere words to describe.

I was undone by what I had seen, but it was far from over.

CHAPTER 27:

GOD COMES DOWN

Outside the garden, Adam and Eve's legacy became one plagued with grief, pain, and sadness. All manner of evil took root quickly, as evidenced by the hate of Cain, leading to the murder of his brother, Abel.

With each passing generation, there was a marked increase in selfishness, violence, and rebellion. There was a void of kindness, compassion, and tender care one for another. Life had become a hard fight for survival that lent itself to an every-man-for-themselves mentality. Carnality was rampant. Paganism, the widely accepted form of worship to false gods, took hold.

The war sin started continued through eons of time. Two kingdoms in conflict, battles for souls raged, and there seemed to be no end in sight.

I saw mankind longing for freedom from the void created when intimacy with God was severed. Those with an awareness of God continued to seek His face, longed for His touch, and listened for His Voice.

Those who did not know Him turned their appetites to fulfilling the lusts and wants of the flesh. They were wildly bent on filling the emptiness in their attempt to forget God.

Both sides lost. All were hurting and hungry for something beyond themselves. Both were crying out for relationship to be restored with our Heavenly Father.

When time passes without an intimate connection with Him, hearts grow weary. Hard. Many became bitter, raising their fist in the face of this unknowable God. They blamed Him for every hardship of their suffering lives.

In answer to the cries of those who kept His Name, He visits. He gives His words to His prophets and reveals His redemption through His Feasts. He refreshed the hearts of His people in myriads of ways, always revealing great love towards them even when they rise up in anger against Him. As the battle between Light and darkness continued to rage, tension mounted.

However, peace radiated from the Kingdom of God. I could sense Heavenly Father was at work in the midst of it. He was establishing His plan, line by line.

Once again, the angel and I were accelerated through time as we passed quickly through the history of heaven. Converging on an appointed time.

When God's order of time was fulfilled, Heavenly Father sends His final answer. He brings hope into the midst of desperation.

His heart was laden with incredible love that had never faded or waxed cold. Redemption of His people will cost Him deeply and bring Him great pain.

Heavenly Father sends Jesus.

CHAPTER 28:

ALL FOR YOU

Jesus humbles Himself and comes to earth in the vulnerable form of an infant. He grows and learns the way of the common people. He sees their grief, senses their desperation, and knows their temptations and failures. He walks with them as one of them.

As He grew, He began His ministry. He walked the earth extending love, healing, and forgiveness to those who received His touch. He poured Truth into His disciples, nurturing their faith, mentoring them in the way of His Father's Kingdom.

He challenged religion, cast out demons, and declared His authority over all things. He submitted His every thought, action, and deed to the will of His Father.

Jesus came to take upon Himself the sin of mankind. He came as the only One who could bring complete redemption to the people and restore all that had been lost. He was our Messiah Ben Joseph, the Suffering Servant.

Many thousands of people were gathered in Jerusalem for the Passover Feast. They never suspected this same Jesus, who was the pure and spotless Lamb of God, was entering the gates of Jerusalem at the exact same time the High Priests were beginning to prepare the lamb for the Passover.

The people cheered and welcomed Him with open arms into Jerusalem. They celebrated Him with a hero's welcome in a procession fit for a King! They laid down their palms branches as they shouted, "Hosanna." There was an expectation for Him to take back Jerusalem and establish an earthly kingdom.

In a very short time, one of His own would betray Him, the people who hailed Him as King would turn on Him, and the crowd would cry out for His death.

I was totally engrossed in the scene before me. Then, I heard cruel laughter and mocking torment spewing out of the clamor. When I looked, I saw the enemy poking and taunting the crowds, fueling the hatred of the people. Some of these people were the very ones Jesus had healed. They had no cause for the bitterness burning within them. They were pawns in the hands of the evil one.

A demonic frenzy was being whipped up, born from the kingdom of darkness. Quickly, the tide was turning, resulting in Jesus being mocked, scorned, beaten nearly to death, tortured, spat on, stripped, and cursed. The evil swirling around him built into a crescendo, ending with Jesus being crucified on a cross, unrecognizable as a human being and misshapen.

I watched in horrific disbelief as these events unfolded.

Then, Jesus looked up into the heavens. When I glanced up, I saw tears pouring down the face of Heavenly Father at the suffering of His beloved Son.

All of heaven was weeping at the injustice being done to the One they adored. The angels were straining to break free to come and rescue Him. These mighty, warring angels could make short order of the demonic brood lurking about. They begged Jesus to give them the command!

Jesus looked into the face of His Father. He saw the depths of Heavenly Father's longing to be restored to mankind, the very ones He created in

His image.

It was clear for all to see. He wanted His people back!

Jesus knew He was the only One who could fulfill this deep desire of His Father's heart. His very lifeblood had to be spilled as the final atonement, the sacrificial Lamb of God, for our sins. It was the price needing to be paid for our complete redemption and restoration.

His decision made, He told the angels to stand down. He surrendered to His Father's will. Sin from all mankind, past, present, and future, came upon Him like a lava flow of sulfuric fire.

My heart was beating wildly in my chest. There was pain so deep I can't describe it. Suddenly, the crowds faded away as I fell at His feet. My face was buried in the dirt covered with His sweat and blood. I heard screaming and wailing, not sounding human. It took me several moments to realize those sounds were coming from me.

There was a burning agony within like I've never known before or since.

I heard someone say, "My child." I looked up through the ugly sobs racking my body.

Jesus was looking straight into my eyes. In that instant, I saw such love that my heart nearly stopped within me. In the midst of His great suffering, He saw me.

He said through pain clenched teeth and gasps for air, "I knew you before the world was formed." His body shuddered, and he rallied the strength to continue, "If you were the only person alive, I would do it all, just for you."

I knew in the core of my being His words were true, and I was undone.

"That is how great your value is to My Father and Me," he continued. "I have made you accepted in the beloved by My blood," he sputtered. And then He died.

I lay face down in the dirt at the foot of His cross for a long time.

He knew. He knew me intimately.

Jesus also knew that without His death, I would never have hope of being restored to His Heavenly Father. I would never know or share in the intimacy He desired with me. Jesus suffered terribly and gave His life willingly so I could once again walk with my Heavenly Father, here and now and forever.

I was torn between bitter tears of sorrow over my sin and tears of thankfulness for such a great love beyond anything I had ever seen.

I don't know how much time passed, but the angel came to my side and gently lifted me to my feet. I couldn't bear to look at that cross again. He gently turned me around.

When he did, I was looking into the face of Jesus!

He was no longer torn, battered, and bleeding. He was clothed in white with a crown upon His head, seated at the right hand of a mighty Throne. He radiated Light and glory and the angels were gathered around singing and declaring, "Holy is the Lamb who was slain."

I heard celebrating behind me. When I turned to look, there was a large throng of people gathered to celebrate all Jesus won for us through His death, His burial, and His resurrection. It's so much more than what I had known before.

I knew I had been saved from my sins. Now He was showing me that through all He suffered, He had won for each of us the power to walk in victory over sin, death, and the grave. Through His resurrection, he defeated the enemy and in so doing, He gave us authority over principalities and powers of darkness.

I was overwhelmed by everything I had seen and experienced, and found myself savoring this sacred and holy time.

I was sitting quietly, taking it all in, when once again, my eyes met with Jesus'. He looked at me with that same love I had seen before He died. He called me to Himself. As I stood before Him, He held something out to me.

As I reach to take them, I saw they were keys. He said, "These are the keys to your heart. I took them back from the enemy. He has no power over you. I'm giving you My
authority over him."

Then, He drew me into His arms as He said to me, "You are Mine."

It's very hard to explain the transforming power His words were to me. I had tasted and relished His love before with childish delight when He held me all those years ago. I had understood more fully His love when I met Him that night on the stairs to my basement.

I had known His love for me, but I had not experienced complete acceptance and belonging because He valued me. My value did not stem from me being some great person; it came from the worth He placed on my eternal soul to go to the lengths He did to redeem me.

In that place of understanding my value to Him, the strongholds of rejection, abandonment, abuse, unworthiness, and feeling unlovable were swept away. As far as the east is from the west, they faded away.

In the days following, we walked and talked together. He met me as I read His Word, and He gave me understanding into His Kingdom. He called out to me, and my heart responded "Abba". This is a Hebrew term of endearment, meaning "daddy".

From that time until now, I've called Him Abba.

I was finding my place within His eternal family. He had made me accepted in the beloved. No longer was I second rate; I was His own.

I felt courage well up within me as He clothed me in Himself. I had been grafted into the Vine, and His life now flowed through me.

My value in His eyes had been engraved upon my heart.

CHAPTER 29:

INTIMACY WITH ABBA

This experience changed my life. By Abba's design, each of us is created for intimacy. When this need goes unfulfilled, our rudimentary attempts to fill this void often lead us into places we hadn't intended to go. The result is usually pain, sorrow, and a broken heart.

This had been the pattern of my own life. I longed for and craved the acceptance of someone who would love, protect, and cherish me. I may not have known it by name, but I could clearly see how all of my life I had longed for intimacy.

At the foot of His cross, I found it.

I couldn't get the image of Abba walking in the garden with Adam and Eve out of my mind. The joy on His face spending time with the apples of His eye. The sweet communion they shared, the child-like freedom to simply be with Him, to know Him, was something I wanted with all my heart.

Thinking back on my childhood, I saw all those brushes with His love were Abba drawing me into this moment. He was revealing Himself to me in so many ways. Filtered through my pain, I didn't know it was Him.

Changes in me began to manifest, grow, and develop as the days marched on. I couldn't spend enough time with Him. We were in a divine dance of a love that I was learning to live in.

I was learning the character and nature of my Abba.

Prayer was not something I did each morning out of any sense of duty. Rather, I lived in the midst of constant conversation with Him. He was my closest friend.

I shared my heart with Him and held nothing back. Every part of me, the good and the bad, was laid before Him with open abandonment. I was learning to walk like His child, who had been firmly grafted into Him. I desired for His life to flow through me.

When I walked in intimacy with Abba, fear had no place. Fear can't stand in His presence. I found my heart filled with courage that didn't come from me.

Knowing He was for me, I was able to embrace a sweet place of rest. Rest from striving, working, and earning His favor.

Believing He would never leave or forsake me, strengthened me to step out and follow Him. I began to understand the cry of Paul's heart when he said "If God be for us, who can be against us?"

The Word of God took on a life of its own. The richness and depth of it was astounding to me. Familiar passages became love letters written by my Abba to me.

I liken intimacy with Abba to the Aurora Borealis. It moves, changes, grows, expands, takes on new colors as it breathes across the universe. Ever in motion by His hand.

I'm carried along by His grace and in His love as He orchestrates my life. I had not known this was even possible up to this point in my life.

I came to realize being with Him eternally wasn't a point in time when I would die and live in heaven with Him someday. No, He wanted to walk with me here and now, in this life, moment by moment. He desired to bring His heaven to earth through the intimacy we shared.

No longer were my hopes and dreams rooted in this world. It seemed empty and shallow to me compared to being in His presence.

He is my world, and I live to bring Him glory and honor. He is my home. I want to walk enveloped in Him.

Salvation is the beginning of our walk in the Kingdom of Light. Intimacy with Him is the life we live, beginning today, for the rest of eternity.

Intimacy with Abba is our highest calling.

CHAPTER 30:

CITIZENSHIP

What makes learning to live in true Godly freedom difficult is learning to see ourselves through Kingdom eyes. It's an entirely different view.

I was learning how to walk intimately with Him, moment by moment. This was an entirely new life for me. I was trusting Abba to lead me through and teach me what I needed to know to live in His presence.

My relationship with Abba had been firmly established. My citizenship had been exchanged from belonging to the enemy of this world to belonging to Him. This is my position in Him, and there was more for me to see.

After WWII, when concentration camp survivors were set free from their prison, many no longer knew who they were. They didn't know where to go or how to live, because they had become indoctrinated to obey their abusers. They had lived so long in bondage that freedom was foreign.

It's much the same for us when we are born into Abba's kingdom. We have to learn who we are and how to live without the abuse of the enemy who held us captive.

Safely tucked in Abba's arms, I was seeing that my past didn't define me. Captivity never defines us. It is an event in time, but it is not who we are.

Through the vision Abba had given me, I had been set free from the lies the enemy had spoken into my mind since childhood. Gaining that freedom was an incredible experience. It was like coming up for a breath of fresh air after being submerged for a very long time.

It helped me see myself as He saw me, and showed me my value and worth to Him. It was the catalyst for learning to live in His freedom, day by day.

As I studied the Word of God, I not only saw Him more clearly, I began to see the Truth of who I am in Him. Having been born into the Kingdom of God, I knew I had been made His child by the definition of birth. The Word of God is rich with terms such as adoption and grafted in, words I love and am so grateful for.

When a child is adopted, they are chosen. They are brought into a family with full rights. The same rights as any member of the existing family. They are not less than anyone. The lines that once separated them are erased through a legal exchange.

They are expected to be an active member of the family and contribute to its well- being. As part of the family, they are to show kindness and love to others in the family and encourage them. They are to abide by the laws of their new household and to honor and obey those in authority over them.

Likewise, when we are adopted into the family of God, our place is secured by the Blood of Jesus. A legal exchange took place for our redemption. His life was given to win ours for His Kingdom. The line of sin that once separated us has been erased, and we now enter into His Throne room with joyful thanksgiving and worship.

We are expected to take our place in the family and contribute to its well-being. We abide under the laws established for our family by the One who is the Head over all, Jesus Christ. Our hearts are set on honoring Him with our lives through obedience.

We now have full legal rights to the Kingdom of God. He withholds nothing from us. We are joint heirs with Jesus, in line with Him to inherit His eternal kingdom.

Even as I write these words, it's reason to pause and let the wonder of those words settle upon me once again. May I never grow weary of hearing them. I am a child of God. Abba is my Father. My brothers and sisters in Christ are my eternal family. He is my home. In Him, I belong.

Day after day, I began uncovering what Abba had to say about me as His child. I wanted my mind renewed with Truth, and I wanted to see myself through His eyes.

I began to make a list of all the verses from the Word of God He was giving me about me. As I read over them, they came alive in me and continued to change my life. He was aligning my thoughts with His. I'll share a few of these powerful and precious words with you:

I am greatly loved by God (Ephesians 2:4)

I am a child of God (John 1:12, Romans 8:14,15 and Galatians 3:26)

I've been adopted (Ephesians 1:5)

I am rescued from darkness into God's kingdom (Colossians 1:13)

I died to the power of sin's rule over my life (Romans 6:1-6)

I am a new creation in Jesus (2 Corinthians 5:17)

Christ lives in me and I live through Him (Galatians 2:20)

I am a joint heir with Jesus (Romans 8:17)

I am accepted in the beloved (Ephesians 1:6)

My life is rooted, built and established in Christ (Colossians 2:6-7)

I am free from condemnation (Romans 8:1)

God supplies all my needs (Philippians 4:19)

I am the temple of God (1 Corinthians 3:16; 6:19)

I am not ruled by fear (2 Timothy 1:7)

I can do all things through Jesus' strength (Philippians 4:13)

I have a sound mind (2 Timothy 1:7)

I am an ambassador (2 Corinthians 5:20)

I am victorious (1 Corinthians 15:57)

I am more than a conqueror (Romans 8:37)

I overcome the enemy by the Blood of the Lamb (Revelation 12:11)

These are not nice quotes from the heart of man. These are Abba's words, the Great I Am, the Most High God over all things.
They are also weapons of war given to stand against the lies, deception, and accusations the enemy uses against me. He is relentless in his attempt to try and lure me back into a place of bondage.

The Word of God is quick and powerful, sharper than any two-edged sword. It has the power to divide between the lies of the enemy and the Truth of the Kingdom of God. It is effective in tearing down the strongholds and renewing our minds. These powerful promises were becoming real to me.

I was seeing in my own life that when I stood in His Truth, letting the Word of God define who I am instead of the world, I am able to walk in His overcoming power.

We discover within those precious pages who we are because of Whose we are. This is part of how we walk in our freedom.

I was discovering my true identity.

CHAPTER 31:

FIGHT FOR HER LIFE

I hid myself in His Word. It was a season where I chose to keep myself on His potters' wheel as a living lump of clay. My cry was for Him to mold and shape me according to His will.

No longer was my focus on the approval of man but rather the smile of my Abba Father. He was the One I longed to please. It was His "Well Done" I lived for each new day.

This time spent alone with Him birthed a quiet confidence in me. I asked Him to make my spiritual roots go down deep so I would be able to withstand the storms of life. He was answering the desire of my heart.

As my identity unfolded, I began to see, we have been given authority through the Blood of Jesus. I saw it in the Word of God, and I had experienced it in my own personal deliverance from darkness. Now I realized I hadn't grasped the depth of what it meant.

It was a source of rejoicing to know the Great I Am lived in me by His Holy Spirit. From His Word, I knew He was far greater than any enemy. I believed He was for me, and nothing could stand against Him. My place in His Kingdom was secure, and I was learning to live in faith in Him as the days marched on.

By this time, I had re-married, and my second child had been born;

another precious baby girl. She was so full of life and a great joy to me.

When she was 10 months old, I took her for her DPT immunization. As expected, she was fussy that night and started running a low-grade fever. I gave her Tylenol and rocked her to sleep. She was restless and sleeping fitfully, so I stayed up and held her.

As the night wore on, her fever began to rise. By the time the doctor's office opened in the morning, it was 103 degrees. They didn't seem too alarmed and instructed me to give her tepid baths, continue the Tylenol, and check back later that afternoon.

Since they weren't overly concerned, I tried not to be either, but something was nagging at my momma's heart. We proceeded with the baths, Tylenol, and lots of rocking.

By 3:00pm, her fever had risen to 104.5 degrees. Now, I was very concerned and once again called the doctor. He agreed to meet me at the hospital. He was having her admitted for observation.

We immediately drove over and sat in the waiting room while her room was being prepared. I noticed she was gazing up at the ceiling, fixated on something. I looked up, trying to find what was mesmerizing her.

When I looked back to her face to try and follow her line of sight, I realized she wasn't seeing anything. Her eyes were blank. There was no life in her.

I screamed for my husband to take her to the emergency room as I went to the desk to call the ER, so they were ready for her. After the call, I was quickly on their heels. As I passed through the doors of the ER, I was stopped by a nurse and pulled into a room. She explained they were working on her and needed information from me.

Within a short time, I would learn that my precious baby girl had gone into full cardiac arrest. They were trying, but not hopeful for her survival, the nurse explained. I needed to be prepared for the worst.

I fell to my knees right there and began to pray. Not the kind of prayer I had been praying the past few hours; these were deep prayers born from the agony of a momma's heart breaking over her baby.

About 20 minutes later, I was told they were able to resuscitate her, but she was in critical condition. They were moving her to the ICU.

Once she was moved, the doctor who had taken her case explained the situation in more detail. The high fever, which had spiked to over 105 degrees, had caused a seizure and her heart had stopped. They were able to resuscitate her, but she was not breathing on her own. She was in a medically induced coma on a ventilator. They were concerned for her mental and physical condition if she did wake up due to the lack of oxygen to her brain.

Interestingly, at the same time this happened, there was a visiting contingent of emergency pediatric physicians touring the hospital. They were there as consultants to bring a pediatric intensive care unit to our local hospital. All of them were in the emergency room when my daughter arrived and were able to assist in her care.

These physicians came to the ICU and were instructing her care team on how to set up equipment for a pediatric patient. They felt it was best she stayed where she was rather than trying to transport her out. I later learned they did not expect her to live through the night and wanted to spare us the expense of the flight.

I was assured she was getting the best care the medical community could provide. I also knew it wasn't enough.

Once everyone left her room, I knelt beside her bed and began warring in the heavenlies over the life and well-being of my child. Prayers flowed out of me in ways I had never prayed before.

This continued for three days. On the morning of the third day, she began to stir. They reduced the medicine and let her try to wake up to see if she would breathe on her own.

Again, they tried to prepare me by telling me she would most likely have severe disabilities, both mentally and physically. Worst case scenario they warned, she would be in a vegetative state the remainder of her life. When they tried to wean her from the ventilator, once again, her heart stopped, and the emergency response team went to work.

They began having conversations about taking her off of life support and letting her pass peacefully. They gave me odds, medical outcomes, and painted a very bleak picture before leaving me to think about it, expecting a decision in the morning.

As I sat stroking her beautiful brown curls, peace and hope filled me. There was a surge of strength I knew wasn't my own. I remembered the promises Abba gave me over this child at her birth. Suddenly, I knew I could not accept their diagnosis as Truth.

I went over and closed the glass doors and pulled the curtain. Then I stood by the bed of this precious little one and began to pray. Only this time it wasn't a request, it was an appeal in the Court of Heaven. I was pleading my case before the Righteous Judge.

I was fighting for her with promises He had given me for her. I warred with the same scriptures Abba spoke over me. I was declaring she had a sound mind and a strong body. I reminded the enemy that greater was He who was holding her than all of the power of darkness in this world. I began asking Abba to send His warring angels to come and fight with me over her so that no weapon formed against her would prosper.

As I prayed these prayers, the same evil presence of the powers of darkness I faced while fighting for my deliverance filled that ICU room. They were mocking me, telling me that my daughter was theirs and they would destroy her.

It was in those moments where the authority I have as a child of God became my only reality.

All the Truths Holy Spirit had been teaching me about who I am in Jesus Christ, and the authority I have over the powers of darkness surged up from deep wells within me. It was very clear that I was fighting for the life of my child.

It was equally clear that I was not fighting alone. I looked up, and there in this room with us leading the battle, was the angel who had come so many times to defend and fight for me. He was standing over my child, sword drawn, fighting fiercely.

Within the hour, the enemy was driven out as dust in the wind. Peace filled that ICU room, and I felt music around me. When I looked up, the angels were worshipping, and songs welled up within me. They are called "High Praises", because they are lifted up to exalt the King of Kings and Lord of Lords for Who He is.

A few hours later, my daughter began stirring again. This time her little eyelashes were fluttering as she was struggling to open her eyes. I asked the nurse to come in and check on her. She, in turn, called the doctor. They had made no changes in her medicine, so they were alarmed she was trying to wake up on her own.

Once again, they were going to try to wean her off the ventilator. I could see in their faces they were doing this for me. They didn't believe anything had changed but were placating an emotional mother's needs.

This time, her breathing remained steady, and her heart kept its regular rhythm. They were shocked and cautiously optimistic. They said the next 24 hours would be telling, as to her mental and physical state.

I stayed by her bed and prayed over her prayers of thanksgiving. I worshipped over her, praising her Creator for His goodness shown to her. I knew this child was consecrated to Him for His purposes. I prayed back the Word declaring she had been formed in my womb and was created for the purpose and glory of God. She did not belong to the enemy; she belonged to Great I Am. Not only would she live, but she would also live each day in the fullness of His calling on her life.

As the sun rose the next morning, and the nurses were changing their shifts, she began to wiggle. In no time, she was moving all of her fingers and toes, and stretching. She looked at me and started to cry, but no sound came out. Tears were rolling down her face, but not a peep out of her. It was so sad to watch.

They discovered that when she was ventilated, her voice box was damaged. It would heal, but it would take some time they said. Most importantly, within a few hours, she sat up, stretched her arms out to me, and tried to scamper close for me to pick her up.

From that day on, she never looked back. She passed every neurological exam, started eating, and was back to her puzzles, which she loved. Within the week, she was moved to a regular room before finally being released.

Over the next few weeks, I began to process what had happened in that hospital room. The enemy had come to rob, kill, and destroy the life of my child. Holy Spirit gave the Word of God to pray over her and told me exactly what to pray in the battle over her life. The enemy was driven back, and Abba prevailed. My daughter was fully restored. 100%. She had no debilitating effects from this episode, and had regained all mobility and mental capacities.

I had witnessed Kingdom authority in action. I saw the result of it in my child every day.
Those prayers declared over her came from the Throne Room of Abba. They were not words of my own making.

Jesus won this authority over the powers of darkness for us through His death, His descent into Sheol, His victory over the enemy and His resurrection. He ascended into heaven, taking those who had waited for their redemption through their Messiah. They were now home with their Heavenly Father.

I was pondering these powerful Truths as I held my daughter until she fell asleep in my arms.

CHAPTER 32:

WEAPONS OF WAR – PART 1

In countries around the world, when new recruits enter the military, they are sent through boot camp. It is a time of conditioning, body, soul, and mind. Among other disciplines, they are taught how to handle the weapons they are given, so they can be successful in combat.

If they are not well versed on how to use their weapons in combat, they will be easily overtaken, taken captive, and ultimately overcome. How criminal it would be to send these valiant and willing young men and women into war without this training.

Likewise, we who bear the Name of Jesus Christ as our Lord and Savior are engaged in the greatest war of all time. The enemy is set on destroying us, our marriage, our children, and our families. He is a thief and a liar, bent on our destruction.

As soldiers for the Kingdom of God, we have been given weapons by Jesus Himself, the Captain of the Host, that empower us to stand in the face of deception and darkness. These weapons of war empower us to rout the enemy out of our lives, our families, and our nation. We must become skilled in their use and allow our hands to be trained for the most crucial war we will ever face.

It is a war worth fighting and fighting well. The spoils of this war are the eternal souls and destinies of those we know and love.

When we are walking intimately with our Abba Father, we know our identity in His Kingdom, and we understand our authority in Jesus Christ, we have the foundation we need for spiritual basic training. Without this foundation, anything we build will fall. We will suffer harm, and the losses will be tragic.

Abba began teaching me about His armor. This is found in Ephesians 6, but also in many other places, including the Psalms. I had heard others praying on the armor of God, and I read these passages many times. However, I hadn't fully understood the power and protection these verses provided for each of us as believers.

After the battle over my daughter, Paul's words in Ephesians took on an entirely new meaning. I began to study with an open heart to see past my own understanding.

There are 6 specific pieces of armor. Each one with a unique design and purpose.

Being a visual person, I looked at numerous pictures of Roman armor and researched a bit of ancient battle strategy. When you have an idea of how the armor of that era was used in hand to hand combat, the scripture passages really come alive!

I have been known to stand in front of a mirror, putting on a piece of clothing as an example of being dressed in each piece. Viewing the armor with those perspectives, I began to see the importance of each piece and understand its purpose more clearly.

It was from these perspectives that the Armor of God became very real to me, personally. My understanding and appreciation for these precious gifts has grown and matured as I have over the years. My thankfulness for Abba's protection does nothing but increase over time.

Paul brings this armor to our attention by telling us that by being clothed in it, we can withstand the evil day. One way of saying this is to be courageous and stand up against all the evil schemes, strategies, and deceitfulness of the enemy that is out to destroy us.

As our world becomes increasingly dark, and evil seems to be on the rise, we have the ability to stand firm and not be shaken. How can we do this? By walking intimately with our King, knowing who we are in Him and being clothed in the Armor of God.

I'm going to share what this armor means to me, as Abba continued to open my understanding.

The Belt of Truth. The first thing that jumps out at me about this piece of Armor is Jesus is the Truth. All Truth needs to be found in Him and apart from Him, no Truth exists. We literally wrap Him and His Truth around us like a belt. He centers us and is at the core of our being. King David prayed he would have Truth in his innermost being. If we are not standing on the foundation of Biblical Truth, we will fall. Every time.

I learned a couple of interesting things about this piece of physical armor. The belt the soldiers wore was a thick piece of leather. However, before they put that on, the would take a long piece of linen and literally wrap themselves in it, kind of like a figure eight pattern around their male private parts.

This was like an ancient version of the jock strap our men wear when they engage in potentially dangerous sports. It protected the tender and vulnerable core being of what made these men. A man's man is a valiant warrior walking in the Truth of the whole counsel of God. This intimate place was to be guarded and covered in Truth.

Over this linen, the thick leather belt was fixed into place. This wide thick leather circled the waist of the soldier, providing protection and stability to his core. There was a long leather skirt that hung down in the front, providing further protection to his manly parts.

The leather continued from the waist up one side of the chest diagonally, crossing over the heart, before proceeding over the shoulder and down his back, attaching to the belt on the backside. Attached to the back of the shoulder was a leather sheath to hold their quiver for arrows and their bow. There was also a sheath for their sword, hanging either from the back strap or their side.

This leather band over the chest provided extra protection over their hearts. Abba wants our hearts to be protected and covered with His Truth. When you are facing the king of darkness and father of lies, this becomes a powerful and important weapon of war!

Often times, the enemy will lure us into his arena of falsehood and deception. In this place, we are confused and overwhelmed with the bombardment of lies and accusations. One of the enemy's tactics of old that he's busy working in our world today is to make wrong look right and right look wrong. When this happens, Truth has then fallen in the streets and is trampled under the feet of the masses who have fallen into deception.

Only the Truth of Jesus Christ will overcome the depths of evil we find ourselves walking in. Only by His Truth will we prevail!

The Breastplate of Righteousness. We are clothed in the righteousness of Jesus Christ, the spotless Lamb of God. Through the power of His Blood, we have been made whole and clean. It's not our own righteousness that allows us to stand in the face of the enemy; it's because we are standing in His finished work.

The enemy is far stronger and smarter than we are as mere flesh and blood. He can and does run circles around us, causing us to chase our own tails but not overcome him. But he is no match for Jesus. The enemy is not able to stand against the One who conquered him eternally, our Lord and Savior, Jesus Christ!

Another tactic of the enemy is to entice us into pride. We get puffed up at times thinking we are all that and more. There are many sources of pride available to the sincere believer. Our knowledge, our understanding of the scriptures, the number of people we minister to, the list is never-ending. When we put our foot in the trap of secretly applauding our own righteousness and strength, we've set ourselves up to be taken down hard.

Only when we are standing covered by the righteousness of the One True Righteous Branch, Jesus Christ, are we able to stand against the enemy. We fight from a surrendered and yielded place to Jesus Christ as the Lord and King over all. He, alone, is God, and beside Him, there is no Savior.

This piece of armor in ancient times fit over the head of the soldier, like putting on a shirt, and rested on their shoulders. It was lined with soft leather and was a strong metal on the outside. This provided protection from the hard blows of the enemy's sword coming down on his shoulders to drop them to their knees.

It also provided protection for their entire torso, including the vital organs. This covered the heart, lungs, and soft belly. Once the heart was covered in Truth, it was protected by the righteousness of Jesus. He is the very air that we breathe.

Shod our Feet with the Gospel of Peace. Standing in the Truth of the gospel, which is the message of the Kingdom of God made available to us through the finished work of Jesus Christ, brings peace in our hearts. This peace passes our natural understanding.

It is the peace of a soldier moving into a raging battle with the bold courage born in a man who knows His Commander intimately, trusts His leadership, and would follow Him anywhere He leads. The soldier enters into the conflict, knowing what he is fighting for; the value of the war he is engaged in. All of these bring peace to him, regardless of the outcome. He has dedicated his very life to die for what he has chosen to live for.

The battle shoes worn by soldiers were durable. Often times they had metal spikes on the sole of the shoe. When an enemy was struck down and fell, the soldiers would literally walk across them with these spiked shoes, bringing about the enemy's demise.

The peace we have in the Kingdom of God through Jesus Christ allows us to stand regardless of the difficult circumstances we are facing. We are able to engage in the battle we face in His peace.

The peace of Abba, which surpasses our own understanding, slices through the enemy's tactics of fear, anxiety, and worry to cut him down. Once he is down, we are crushing him under our feet as we walk in the pure and holy peace only intimacy with Abba can provide.

When the enemy is defeated, peace reigns in our hearts, our homes, and our nations.

CHAPTER 33:

WEAPONS OF WAR – PART 2

The Shield of Faith. Faith is choosing to believe Abba above anything else. It's resting in the firm belief that He is God; we are not. His ways are higher than ours, and His thoughts far exceed our abilities to reason. He is the Great I Am, the Only Wise God, and besides Him, there is no Savior. He is the Alpha and Omega, and our lives are hidden in Him. What He says, goes.

The power of the shield of faith lies in the knowledge that our eternal destiny is rooted in Someone so much greater than ourselves, the King of all kings and the Lord over all lords, Jesus Christ. Faith roots us firmly, empowering us to appropriate the victory He won over sin, death, and the grave.

When you think about the damage a fiery arrow being thrust into you can cause, the value of this shield becomes apparent. The enemy would take an arrow and cover it with pitch or tar. Sometimes, poison would be added. The arrow would then be lit on fire and launched at the soldiers. The pitch or tar burned slowly and was gooey. If the arrow hit you, it didn't have to be a fatal hit. The tar or pitch would stick to where it hit and would continue to burn.

The soldier's shield was made out of wood covered in thick pieces of leather. There would be a metal band around the edges to re-enforce it as well as a metal band around the center. Sometimes the front-facing metal band would have a spike on it or be rounded to be used as a human battering ram.

The shields would be soaked in water before battle to help protect them from the fiery arrows. When the arrows struck their shield, the moisture would help extinguish the flames.

Often times, the soldiers would stand shoulder to shoulder with their shields held in front of them. This had the effect of building a human wall. The troops would move forward as one large group, advancing into enemy territory to accomplish the task at hand.

This unity in battle was a scary display of power to behold. Many enemies fled at the sight of it. It also made it difficult for the enemy to penetrate and attack individuals.

These fiery darts of the enemy are how we are wounded so deeply. We are hurt by peoples' actions or words, we make decisions out of fear, or we're driven by the approval of man. There's a myriad of ways we make our hearts vulnerable to attack.

The enemy is constantly launching his fiery darts at us. He knows exactly where to aim to bring us down. When one of these fiery darts hits its mark, it opens up a deep, ragged gash in us. The goo that sticks to us continues to burn. These ugly wounds often get infected, fester, and poison the whole system. For a soldier on the battlefield, this is deadly.

When we're down, the enemy then takes full advantage of our weakness. He doesn't relent. Rather he hits us again and again in the same wound as he tries to inflict more damage. This is the nature of war.

Faith is believing Abba. It is trust in Him without borders. Faith requires I believe what He says about me and my circumstances rather than what I see with my natural understanding. This is why we must know who we are in the Kingdom of God and what Abba says about us. In this way, we are like the shield when it is drenched in the water before battle. The Word of God, Holy Spirit is often referred to as our

Living Water. When our lives are immersed in Him, and we have soaked in His presence, the fiery darts of the enemy have no effect on us because we are standing strong in believing faith.

This shield of faith prevents fiery darts of lies, accusation, unbelief, fear, anxiety, depression and torment, just to name a few, from ever getting close enough to stick in us. When we are getting hit hard, our brothers and sisters in Christ stand over us with their shield held high to protect and defend us in battle. This gives us time to get back up on our feet and move out once again.

The incredible thing about this piece of armor is that it extinguishes ALL the fiery darts of the enemy. All is a very little word with a great big meaning. This piece of armor doesn't extinguish some of the fiery darts. No, it has the power to extinguish them all.

Every. Last. One.

The Helmet of Salvation. This piece of armor is fashioned and designed specifically to protect our mind, the place where all beliefs are birthed and subsequent actions are launched from. Our mind is the ultimate battleground.

Our minds are being assaulted 24/7 through media, TV shows, movies, friends, family, and our own past wounds. These are venues filled with lies to throw us off spiritual balance, to trip us up, and cause us to fall. The enemy is unceasingly whispering his lies to us, luring, tempting, and taunting us out of the arena of faith into his arena of deception.

When we believe in our mind the enemy's lies, we follow his trail of destruction that always leads to death. Our mind determines our path. This is where our choices are made.

When we enter into salvation through Jesus Christ, our mind is renewed. Everything has changed, including our thoughts.

The things that I used to find entertaining have now lost their attraction, especially the vile things of the world. We take on the mind of Jesus

Christ. We love what He loves, we follow Abba as Jesus, doing and saying nothing apart from His Father's leading.

When we are clothed with the helmet of salvation, we are actively filling our minds with the Truth of Jesus Christ. We believe what He says, and we accept His Truth about our new identity in Him.

For the soldier, protecting his head was crucial in battle. A soldier without a helmet wouldn't last long. If our mind is not clothed with the helmet of salvation, we won't last long either. The enemy will chew us up and spit us out.

This piece of armor was crafted specifically for each soldier. Great lengths were taken to make sure it fit him perfectly. The helmet covered his entire head, his neck and rested on top of the breastplate of righteousness.

It was hard on the outside to deflect the many blows yet soft on the inside to buffer and absorb the shock. It was critical that it fit well so it would not be knocked off in the fierceness of the battle around him.

Renewing our minds can be a fierce battle with our own flesh at times. We are told to take every thought captive so we can obey Jesus. The enemy knows full well that if he can take hold of our minds, he has scored a great victory towards our destruction.

The battle over our minds can be one of the fiercest, but is one worth the fight.

The Sword of the Spirit. By pure definition, this is the Word of God, the Holy Bible, the whole counsel of God from Genesis to Revelation. This is a precious gift and the foundation for all we believe.

It is the final authority. The absolute Truth for all who choose to live in the Kingdom of God. We do well when we submit to the whole counsel of God. This is the righteous standard we live by, not from a place of legalism to the letter but from a yielded place of surrender in loving God His way, through His Spirit.

It contains the rich history of our faith, gives us prophetic insight in days to come and is the oracle of God Himself revealing His nature, character, and desires for those who call upon His Name.

Sadly, we often treat it as a mere suggestion or a storybook. This plays right into the enemy's hands, and he delights when the Word of God is deemed ineffective for today's problems. After all, he whispers, it's so old and archaic, how can it be relevant to modern times? This is his supreme lie.

If you want to tear down a structure, regardless of its size, simply destroy its foundation. When you've accomplished that feat, everything built upon it will crumble into a messy heap. Is it any wonder the Word of God is under such attack, being questioned, sliced and diced and mocked?

The Word of God is to be revered, trusted, and obeyed from a heart surrendered to Holy Spirit. It's not a battering ram to beat others up with; it's alive and living and more powerful than a two-edged sword to divide Truth from lies. It's imperative we know it well.

For a soldier, his sword was his weapon of offense. He would never dream of using it against his fellow soldiers. It was a weapon wielded against the enemy, those who came to bring destruction by stealing his land, harming his family, and seeking to kill him.

He used his sword skillfully and with great wisdom. He trained and practiced his art with great discipline. The soldier knew his ability with the sword would be the difference between life and death for himself and those he loved.

This was the love Abba put in my heart for His Word.

The Armor of God is unlike physical military weapons of war. They are cold, hard, and lifeless. The armor of God is alive!

It ebbs and flows as each piece moves and melds with the other. They interact with the other, accenting and strengthening each one like a well-conducted symphony. The beautiful sounds they release are for the sole purpose of providing protection from all of the enemy's advances against us.

Its value is immeasurable.

For me, it wasn't a matter of simply learning the pieces of armor. No, like a good soldier, I needed to be trained in their use. I needed to understand the power each piece held and its value in warfare. I had to know instinctively how to wield them all both offensively and defensively.

Freedom depends on it.

CHAPTER 34:

CHAINED IN THE BAY

I was facing a time of discouragement. I loved my intimate times with Abba and all that He was teaching me from His Word. It seemed like I wasn't able to move forward. I felt stuck somehow, and I didn't understand why.

As I was talking to Him and asking for His wisdom, He showed me something I've never forgotten. It has served me well for many years, and I want to share it with you.

I saw myself treading water in a beautiful bay. In my heart, I knew that I needed to get to the shore because there were things the Lord wanted me to do there. I had been struggling to get there but wasn't making any progress. Frustrated, I began looking for the reason I couldn't move towards the shore.

Looking down into the clear water, I saw a chain. I followed it with my eyes and realized it led to an iron collar around my neck. I pulled at it, but it would not budge. Panic was beginning to settle in when I realized I was somehow chained to the ocean floor.

I tried to follow the chain into the water to see where it would lead. I could see it go down and then form a "U" shape. I followed to where I thought it would re-surface and found myself staring into many faces of people I knew. Some I didn't recognize by face or name, but I knew who they were. They were also treading water.

When I looked more closely, I realized they also had an iron collar around their neck. Then, the full realization of the situation settled upon me.

These people were the faces from the pain I had endured, some from my worst nightmares. They were all chained to me in the middle of this bay. These were not people I wanted anywhere near me, let alone in a dire situation as we were in.

Fear started to overtake me as I was panic-stricken to get free. I began clawing at the collar around my neck, but when I stopped paddling, I would start to sink. The people all looked hopeless and dull, unaware of the danger we were in. They seemed to have accepted their lot. I was having none of it.

I looked up and cried out, "Abba, help!"

I felt Him draw near. I didn't understand what I was doing here with these horrible people. I told Abba I needed to get to shore because I knew there were things He wanted me to do, but I couldn't move. I asked Him to set me free and take me away from this place. I was crying hard by now.

"Child," He spoke to my heart, "Look at Me." I stopped struggling and looked into His face.

He spoke gently but firmly, "The chains are created by your unforgiveness. They are binding you to these people and keeping you from fulfilling the work I have for you. You must choose to forgive them and set yourself free."

Immediately, I was afraid. I had heard many sermons saying if I truly forgave these people, I needed to invite them into my inner circle as friends. If I couldn't do that, I hadn't really forgiven them.

Because of this teaching, I feared forgiveness.

I looked back into Abba's face. I saw such love for me and compassion.

He said, "Trust Me. I will give you strength."

I followed the heaviest chain from around my neck out to the face it was attached to. There was the man from my childhood who had brought me so much hurt. My stomach was sick when I looked into his face.

After a moment, I was surprised to realize there was no bitterness towards this man. That had been broken off of me. What I did feel was a desire for vengeance, not by my hand but by Abba's. I wanted Abba to bring this man into the dust where this man's hurtful acts had taken me.

Out here treading water in this bay, I was seeing this man differently. I was seeing a man bound for eternal separation from God, without hope and in despair. A man who was broken himself.

There wasn't a natural desire to forgive Him. It was a choice. I had to choose to set my will to forgive him. I repented for the unforgiveness I held against this man and asked Abba's forgiveness for harboring a vengeful attitude towards him. Suddenly, I didn't want to bring him harm or see him hurt.

In an instant, the chain tethering us together dissolved and he was carried out to sea by the current. I never saw him again.

This scene repeated itself as I went from face to face, choosing to forgive and repenting for my unforgiveness. Each time, the chains fell off, the people were swept out to sea and disappeared from my view.

One of the faces I saw was my mother's. She looked lost and alone. This surprised me because the anger wasn't visible.

Over the years, I tried to have conversations with my mother over the events of the past. These times did not go well. She was unable to speak on the level necessary to bring healing. However, I had learned my mother had also suffered sexual molestation as a young girl.

Her voice had also gone unheard by her own mother and father. When she had tried to talk with her own mother, it became a quarrel about whose side of the family had caused this hurt. She, too, had been wildly accused of lying. The same words inflicted upon her were inflicted upon me. All the time, her pain went unaddressed. As was the custom of this era, it was quietly shoved under the rug. She was forbidden to speak of it again.

My mother's pain had been buried deep within her. She carried it even now. I realized this made it impossible for her to bear facing mine all those years ago. Her inability to help me caused a hardness in her heart towards me. She expected me to carry the pain as she had, as if this was the normal state of affairs for all young girls. This was all she had known.

I forgave my mother with tears pouring down my face. The enemy had stolen so much from us. We had lost the sweet mother-daughter relationship. Instead, we were estranged from one another. I released my mother into the peace of Jesus Christ, asking Him to heal the brokenness within her. I knew she was being held in Abba's arms as she floated out to sea.

Finally, there were no more chains holding me in that place. I looked down, and the iron collar slipped off and fell to the bottom of the bay. I easily swam to shore and fell on the beautiful beach with joy in my heart.

Abba came and sat with me on that beautiful beach. He spoke to me about how unforgiveness binds us to folks and their sins. He can't bring the corrections necessary without it affecting all those who are tethered together. His work is thwarted by unforgiveness.

I also saw clearly how each of us have a story. We bear the mark of other people's hurt, wounds, and pain. I wasn't responsible for how these people arrived at the place in life, but I now saw them through different eyes.

I saw broken people struggling to live life from deep behind walls they had created for their own protection. Living from this walled off place is distorted, outside of reality. They may have become successful in the eyes of the world, but their souls were captive to darkness and torment. These people were not evil, but evil had taken up residence within them in varying degrees.

Forgiveness of others doesn't ensure the broken relationships would or should be restored. Sometimes, we must remove ourselves from toxic situations.

Too many people stay in abusive relationships with the false hope things will change. This can be a deadly decision, bringing much harm to themselves and to those they are responsible for. Abuse should never be tolerated in any relationship.

As believers, we should be willing to support those who are fleeing such situations without judgment. I learned to be compassionate, kind, and listen to others as they shared their stories. We must acknowledge abuse exists within the body of Christ, and we should not turn a blind eye or cover it with platitudes. Too many abusers are able to continue their destructive work when good people remain silent.

I had to give myself the grace to know I wasn't strong enough to stand in the midst of those who chose to dwell in the enemy's camp. Not yet, anyway. I needed to be a safe distance from those who had brought me great harm. This took humility to admit my weakness. I had to let go of others and trust Abba for the healing work He was doing in me, to make me strong.

Each one of us has our own story. Each of us is also responsible for what we do with our story. There is no freedom in pointing the finger at those who caused our hurt. There's no healing to be had in blame.

I learned that through forgiveness, I was able to see each living person as an eternal soul with an eternal destiny, rather than through the filter of my pain. When I was able to see them as human beings, I was able to walk as an overcomer.

This did not remove the guilt of their actions or minimize the pain they had inflicted; it enabled me to let them go. I was able to lift them up and lay them in the hands of Abba for His will to be done.

Forgiving those who have deeply hurt us is not about how we feel. If we live and function from the arena of feelings, we will be defeated every time. This will lead us into the enemy's playground of unforgiveness, along with a myriad of other traps he has laid. Unforgiveness opposes the new Kingdom we are living in.

As believers, we are called and equipped to live and fight from the arena of faith. Faith that is built upon the Word of God; His Truth. Faith that stands upon the Rock of Jesus Christ will not be moved, regardless of how we feel.

I wanted to live victoriously, and now I knew this was the path to get there. Freedom is found in forgiveness.

CHAPTER 35:

PRAYER OF THE WARRIOR

With a clean heart free from unforgiveness, I continued studying the Word. It seemed to me the entire purpose of the Armor of God is to equip us to be able to stand in prayer. Paul concludes his writings about the armor by telling us to pray at all times in the Spirit. We're to stay alert and persevere in prayer, interceding for God's people. I wasn't really sure what this meant.

I was thinking about the prayers that came deep from my spirit over my sick baby. They had been a far cry from the prayers I had prayed in the past. I saw more clearly how these were the intercessions of the Spirit, fighting in the heavenlies with authority.

I realized that, simply put, intercession is the prayer of the warrior. It is standing in the gap in battle over those Abba has given you charge of. It can be a person, a group of people, a city, or a nation. It is a divine assignment given by His hand. These were the prayers poured out over my child.

The basis of intercession is identification. It is not a prayer prayed "at" people. I've prayed more of those kinds of prayers than I ever would want to admit. Now, I'm very sorry for each one.

It's not the long list of my needs, which in true transparency were mostly my wants. It is good that we speak with Abba about everything that concerns us. He is attentive to our needs, and it matters to Him. I had to learn that He wasn't a good luck charm, aimed at giving me whatever I wanted because I asked. Sometimes, He said no.

Intercession is none of those things. It is unique.

Intercession is taking your place alongside people and praying them through as one. Their needs, their struggles, and their victory are dearer to you than your own. You lay down your life for them because Abba has planted this amazing love in you over them.

What also sets intercession apart from other forms of prayer is you are standing where Abba is telling you to stand. You stand clothed in His armor, with your Sword drawn, standing between the enemy and the people you are fighting for.

You are declaring the enemy must go through you to get to the people you are standing over. You are setting up a hedge of protection around these people; one the enemy can't penetrate.

Abba may be moving these people to a place of safety, He may be calling them to a place of repentance over sin, or He may be wooing hearts to Him in salvation. This is His work to accomplish. The intercessor simply stands in a place of protection, so this work can be accomplished.

These battle lines can be fierce, and it is essential that you have been called to it. When you are called, then Abba gives you everything you need.

One day, as I was spending time with Abba, He gave me eyes to see into the spiritual realm. Abba came and took me up on top of a high mountain. At the top, there was a narrow crevice. From this crevice, a path meandered down to two valleys below, one on either side of the mountain.

As we stood in that crevice, I looked down into the valley on my right. I saw hundreds, if not thousands, of white tents set up with lots of activity around open fires. The women were cooking, children were running around playing, the men were doing all sorts of chores: building, chopping wood, tending animals, and digging up the ground to plant crops.

It was a busy community; a peaceful scene. Casual and comfortable was the tone.

Abba laid a hand on my shoulder and turned me around to face the valley lying in the other direction. With the joy of the peaceful scene fresh in my mind, I wasn't prepared for the scene far below us. A gasp escaped before I could stop it.

This valley was filled with swarming black creatures. They were oozing black tar, smelled like death, and were gruesome looking. Some were massive in size while others looked like crosses between humans and animals. Others had blood dripping from their mouths where they were tearing apart wild animals and eating them raw.

Still others were grouped together and were sparring with each other. There was no mercy shown, and they killed their own, gloating over their conquest. There isn't a way to convey the atrocities being committed in this camp. It was a terrifying scene to behold.

As we stood there, one contingent of gruesome creatures began to rally themselves. They were picking up an assortment of brutal looking weapons. They were pushing and shoving, cursing and mocking each other as they started a slow but steady march. They were huge in size and strength. Their feet sounded like a drumbeat as they fell hard upon the ground. Even from this distance, I could feel the earth tremble.

They were marching directly towards the crevice where we were standing. It was the only way across the mountain.

As I looked back into the valley of white tents, it was apparent they had no idea what was marching their way. I was filled with panic. I wanted to run down the mountain to warn the people of what was coming. It was frightening. They wouldn't stand a chance against this vile army coming their way.

I looked at Abba and saw immense compassion in His eyes. He said to me, "I'm calling you to stand in the gap over My people. You have been equipped and trained to hold back this demonic host from bringing harm to those who are unprepared. You have everything you need to stand. Take courage. You are not alone. I will never leave you nor forsake you."

He had me stand in this crevice facing the tents, my back to the enemy. This seemed all wrong to me, but He said, "Trust Me. I am your rear guard."

In a short time, I could feel the enemy drawing close behind me. They were close enough to see me and began to curse at me. I stood in the crevice, clothed in the Armor of God, and began speaking His Word that flooded my mind. I don't know how long this went on, but they finally retreated back to the valley floor, warning me they would be back another day with more of them.

I had stood, but I was shaking head to toe. I didn't feel valiant; I simply felt scared.

Then, I heard a noise above me and looked up. I saw the same angel, along with his fellow warriors, who had fought over me for my deliverance. They were heaving from the battle that had taken place behind me. Truly, I was not alone!

Looking at this angel, I realized these were the warriors Abba sent to be my rearguard in that place of intercession. They had routed the enemy and drove them back into their dark valley.

My intercession had not been to face the enemy and stop them from advancing. Not this time, anyway. My place of intercession was for the people in the valley to wake up!

I learned a valuable lesson that day.

When I'm standing in Abba's will from a place of obedience to His call, His glory is released by my simply showing up. My standing where Abba told me to stand was sufficient to stop the enemy. Abba took care of the rest.

There are two kingdoms at war. The battle rages and the enemy is relentless. Day and night, night and day, they are waging war against the Saints of the Lamb.

Jesus, as the Captain of the Angelic Army, is the One who orchestrates each member of the body of Christ by His Holy Spirit. It is essential to walk in obedience to Him. I am safe only in the center of His will.

Our King and Lord has not left us defenseless. In Him, we have everything we need to be more than conquerors.

We have been given His authority to walk as overcomers through His precious blood. Clothed in His armor and surrounded by His hedge of protection, we are able to stand.

We must be relentless in fighting the good fight of faith, persevering to the end.

CHAPTER 36:

MOTIVES MATTER

All of these lessons were affecting my desires for the kind of life I wanted to live. As a mother of small children, I knew what I didn't want to be to them. But I had no idea how to raise my family differently from what I had known. I spent a great deal of time in prayer, asking Abba to teach me and lead me in His ways for my everyday life.

As my heart was being healed and strengthened, I was being changed. Freedom affects all of our relationships; how we speak, our actions, and how we love.

I had to learn that the ways of the Living and Holy God are often counter-cultural. The world is not the trendsetter for believers in Jesus Christ.

I'm not called to create cultural counterfeits to look like the world, so Christianity is appealing to the flesh. I am called to hold out an entirely new way of living in the Kingdom of Light.

This new life far surpasses what this world can ever be. We seek the heart of God to bring His glory and establish His Kingdom from heaven to earth according to His will.

When we choose to obey God with all our heart, often times a violent conflict with the powers of darkness that rule the earth will follow. This spiritual war makes no sense to the natural mind because it cannot understand this timeless battle is for eternal souls.

Those who do understand what is at stake have willingly yielded their lives, even unto dying horrible deaths rather than denounce the Name of Jesus Christ. This martyrdom continues into our modern day in countries around the world. Again, dying for the Name of Jesus Christ makes no sense to the natural mind who doesn't know Him as their Savior and Lord. Living for Him can be equally as difficult in a different way.

We are His Ambassadors, sent to represent His Name wherever our feet take us throughout the day. As such, it matters how we live.

I had heard many times the old adage: The end justifies the means". In the Kingdom of God, the end does not justify the means. The means are important to Abba. He searches and tries our hearts every step of the way. Our motives matter to Him.

When I found myself in a pickle, I would cry out for Him to deliver me. My motive was my desire to be removed from hard situations. I don't like conflict or strife and wanted Him to get me out of anything difficult quickly.

Abba taught me that my deliverance from the situation was not His first priority; my heart was. He cared that I was in difficulties, and it mattered to Him how I handled the situation. The character I exhibited as we walked through the valley together was revealed and it exposed unsightly things in me.

These were times of maturing and establishing me in His ways. I learned, over time, to lean into these opportunities to be pruned, formed, and fashioned after Him. I came through each one stronger and looking more like my Abba.

I would have to remind myself: I can't do any of this Kingdom living on my own, nor does He expect that from me. He tells me clearly, that apart from Jesus and His Spirit living through me, I can do absolutely nothing for His Kingdom.

The call to us who bear His Name is to live holy before Him. This isn't self- righteous legalism that makes others feel small. It's not judgmental condemnation. I had suffered many times under this heavy hand of what man defines as holy. I've seen others hurt as well.

Man's attempt to be holy from his own carnal nature is always a recipe for disaster. It leaves many wounded, and they often walk away. This made Jesus very angry, and He responded with harsh condemnation of this attitude. Self-made holiness is not born from Abba's heart.

Holiness is born out of a loving, intimate relationship with our Heavenly Father. It is my relationship with Abba changing me into His image.

Similar to a young boy who wants to spend all his time with his daddy. he dresses like him, stands like him, uses His lingo, and picks up his mannerisms. More than anything in the whole wide world, he wants to be just like his daddy when he grows up.

Why? Because the little boy loves his daddy with all his heart.

Likewise, when we spend intimate time with our Heavenly Father, learning His character, seeing His justice, knowing His ways, we want to grow up to be just like Him.

Why? Because we love Him with all our heart, soul, mind, and strength.

The disciples of Jesus were changed in the time they spent with Jesus. He showed them a different life, a life that was counter-cultural to the one they had known. They learned many things, one of which was how to be in the world but not of it.

One prayer that rose up from my heart was, "Abba, make sin increasingly sinful to me." I wanted sin to lose it savor and enticement. I did not want it to rule my life because I saw clearly how sin opposes holiness.

When I stop and consider the great lengths Abba went to for my redemption, it is easy to see the afront willful sin is to His Kingdom. The price paid for me to be free from the law of sin was the Blood of His precious Son. Now that I have accepted His sacrifice for my own salvation, choosing to sin is like spitting in the face of Abba and trampling under my feet the sacrifice Jesus made.

I wanted to understand holiness from Abba's heart. As I pressed into this, He made it known that holiness isn't something I do in my own strength or reasoning. It flows from who I am in Him; it is part of my new identity. It abides in my spirit when I am yielded and tender to His ways.

The enemy was working against these truths, not wanting them to take root in my life. He often works in his temptations for us to take back the ownership of our lives, making our flesh the god of ourselves. This is the culture of the world, and we can see where it leads us. Everyone does what is right in their own mind.

When we agree with culture and allow it to permeate our lives, it allows the enemy the legal right to do two things. First, he can openly and violently attack us. Second, he can use us as pawns for evil purposes.

The temptation to be our own god is a trap we want to stay out of. How well I remember this from the vision Abba had shown me. This desire was the source of Lucifer's fall from heaven. That didn't end well for him. I didn't want to go there.

We must stay the course. We must walk in obedience to the Word of God from hearts that are yielded and tender towards Abba. We must choose to walk in holiness before Him, upholding His righteous decrees and playing within His boundaries for His people.

Again, Abba reminded me that my intimate relationship with Him comes first above all things. From our sweet communion, I want to learn to walk in His ways.

CHAPTER 37:

ONE BODY, MANY GIFTS

When we are born into the Kingdom of God, each of us is given spiritual gifts. These are precious, rich treasures. They are wired into our being and activated by Holy Spirit. They are His calling on our life.

Just like when we're born into this world, we have personalities and things we are naturally good at. We can learn many skills and develop strengths as we grow up. However, gifts are those things that come easily to us because they are part of our DNA.

Through the Blood of Jesus, old things are passed away, and we are made new. We inherit new spiritual DNA, which includes supernatural gifts and strengths to be used for His Kingdom.

When you meet people who are fulfilling what they were called to do, you can see the passion, joy, and power in their lives. They are encouraging to be with.

There are many spiritual gifts, and we can learn to function in all of them to some degree. However, there will be one or two that we supernaturally excel in. Some people are gifted in music, others athletically and still others at teaching. These gifts flow out of the core of their being.

It's important for us to know our gifts. They are a part of your identity in Jesus Christ.

Our gifts are also key to knowing our destiny in the Kingdom.

I had seen the evil side of life as well as some pretty amazing things in the Kingdom. People wanted to hear my story. My own emotional immaturity didn't know how to handle this attention. Quickly, it began to puff me up, and before too long, I was full of myself. I didn't see people for where they were on their journey of faith. I was critical, harsh, and arrogant. I joined my hand with pride.

Regardless of how much we learn from studying the Word of God, there are some things in life that only time will mature. Handling the attention of man, without it being a trap for your feet, is one of them. I hadn't learned this lesson yet. But in short order, Abba had had just about enough of this proud arrogance from me.

One morning, I was in my upstairs prayer place talking with Abba. I sensed all was not well, and it grieved my heart. I asked Him what I had done; I truly wanted to know.

In an instant, He came in such power I was on my face on the floor without knowing how I got there. I could sense His hot displeasure and yes, His anger. I felt that if He didn't look away from me, I would surely die. It was heavy upon my heart and crushing in my spirit. He said to me, "Do not touch My glory!"

I instantly saw what I had done. The hard words were exposed along with the judgment I had rendered against people. I was sick to see what I had done.

This was when I knew, beyond any doubt, that our motives matter to Him. I was saying and doing all the right things, but inwardly I was arrogant and proud. I was disgusted with myself. How could I ever think any of the spiritual healing I had experienced had come from me?

My heart was broken, and I was crying very hard at what I had seen in me. In my ignorance, I was hurting good people.

Immediately, I began to repent. I confessed my sins, asking for His forgiveness and cleansing. I laid there a very long time as peace began to seep into my heart and restore me once again.

I've never forgotten that moment. It was permanently etched upon my soul. That day, Abba drew a line in my soul. One I knew I never wanted to cross again. He is a loving Father, but when we transgress against His holiness, daring to touch His glory, it is a fearful thing to fall into His hands.

What does this have to do with our spiritual gifts?

To manipulate or use any of the spiritual gifts through our flesh is terribly dangerous. It is touching God's glory and claiming ownership of His works. If we persist on this path, it will lead us into occult activity. Using spiritual gifts through our carnal flesh is denounced by the Word of God with severe consequences to any who dabble in occultism. It's throwing the door wide door for the enemy to come in and bring destruction. The strong Biblical warnings must be heeded.

From that place of repentance, I rose up with humility and compassion born of His Spirit. No longer did I elevate me and my gifts over others. Rather, I learned to value the gifts of my spiritual family, and humbly receive their work in my life. I was the piece of iron needing to be sharpened by them.

I can say now from a true heart that I've come to love those opportunities to grow in grace. There is power when others are walking freely in their calling, and I'm grateful for them ministering to me.

From this lesson, I came to know that one gift is not more valuable than another. All of the gifts are inter-dependent upon one another. This is how the body of Christ is to function and remain healthy. We are to build each other up in our gifts as we cover and uphold each other in our weaknesses.

Since that time, I've had the opportunity to spend time with various denominations, cultures, and nationalities. I come away from each of these experiences enriched! It gives me a glimpse of what the first church may have looked like before division drove us apart by our man-made rules and regulations.

Each one of these gatherings has a part of the truth, but none have it all. Each one has considerable strengths, yet is greatly lacking in some areas. These weaknesses minimize their effectiveness in being what they desire to be.

How my heart longs for us to come together in unity and value the gifts each one brings to the Holy table of the Almighty God! We could learn so much from one another if we would humble our hearts and walk together in genuine humility.

When we are all walking in our gifts, in submission to Holy Spirit, we are an unstoppable force for Abba's Kingdom. Can you imagine what we could accomplish if we would grab hold of this Truth and walk together as Abba designed? These gifts are powerful because Abba is the source of each one. His gifts empower us to serve others by being who we were created to be.

As a child, I learned a valuable lesson from an elderly farmer. He was "old school", and I loved to hear his stories. This day, he was telling me about plow horses. He took me out to his barn and was showing me the old, leather harness he had used for many years on his farm.

He took one off the wall - it had a name stamped in the leather. He went on to explain to me that a good farmer understands the need for each horse to have its own harness. It must fit them perfectly, because plowing up hard ground is hard work.

If the harness didn't fit right, it would rub a sore on the horse's shoulder. The plowing couldn't be stopped, so day after day, wearing an ill-fitting harness agitated the sore. It had no time to heal. If the farmer didn't stop and make a harness that fit properly, this infection would eventually kill the horse.

It is much the same with our spiritual gifts. It's important to take the time to study the Word of God to discover what they are. Ask Holy

Spirit to reveal which ones are yours. Ask those you trust to help you understand which gifts they see in you. There are great resource materials describing the gifts, how they work, and how to help you discover yours.

As I mentioned before, knowing your gifts is key to knowing your destiny in the Kingdom. It removes the temptation to compare yourself with others because these gifts you've been given are uniquely yours. You were created to walk in them, and they fit you perfectly.

As I walked with honor and respect for the gifts I saw in others, I was learning how to walk in the gifts I had been given. I didn't come to discern this by myself; many others spoke this over my life and helped me understand what this meant.

One of my gifts is that of a "seer". You may know what this means Biblically, but I didn't. I began to study to understand that seers are given the ability to "see" things from heaven's perspective, as Abba chooses to reveal them.

Understanding this gift helped me understand what I'd experienced during my deliverance. I hadn't been startled when I saw the angels fighting for me in the battle for my freedom. Nor was I shaken that an angel spoke to me and encouraged me through that difficult time, because I had seen them from my earliest memories.

I thought about the countless times Abba had shown me lessons through creation during my childhood. I said in earlier chapters that Abba had raised me. This is what I meant by that statement. He spoke to me about how to treat other people, instructed me about right and wrong. He gave me a strong sense of justice and courage to speak Truth. He gave me the guidance I sorely lacked in my life.

Not only had I not understood this gift, neither did the people in my life. I'm sure they didn't know what to do with the things I shared, before I learned not to. Their reaction was to shut me down and silence my voice. They said I was crazy and even demon possessed.

A genuine seer gift comes only from Abba. It is His choice as to what He reveals, when and why. Sometimes the things He reveals are to be spoken. However, in my walk I've found this gift to be used mainly for intercessory prayer.

I believe with all my heart, each of us hears from Abba. This is the desire of His heart, to walk intimately with us. Intimacy is largely founded on communication. When we take time and still our hearts before Him, we will learn to discern His still small voice.

When my children were young, they would say, "Momma, I don't hear God talk to me." I would ask them, "When you wanted to pinch your sister, what happened in your heart?"

They would look at me and say, "Well, I really wanted to pinch her, but then I knew it was wrong, so I didn't." I would ask them, "How did you know it was wrong?"

They would reply, "Well, it was like I heard a voice telling me not to do that even though I really wanted to." I would hold them close and say, "That was God talking to you, telling you not to do that naughty thing to your sister."

They would smile and go on about their day. They were encouraged to pay more attention to those times when God was speaking to them. Many times, they would run back to tell me stories of how God had revealed Himself to them. They were excited about this.

I would say the same for each of us.

Abba is often speaking, but we may not be recognizing His voice or taking time to listen. The world has done a good job of telling us this is our inner self, our conscience, or an "energy force".

To me, this says even the world understands the interaction God has with us, but they choose not to accept it, so they re-label it. The Holy Spirit is a still small Voice that speaks to us many times throughout the day. We have to train ourselves to be still and know Him. This can take some time to develop; enjoy this time with Him.

Then there are times He speaks, and we don't want to hear Him. There are numerous reasons, but it usually comes down to that we want to go our own way. We don't want to hear because we don't want to be told no. I've noticed that in our culture, we have an issue with being told no. Sometimes, Abba's answer is no. We must choose to trust Him.

Be courageous in finding the way Abba speaks to you. For some, He gives songs. For others, they hear Him in their service to others. Some hear Him as they prepare to teach. Regardless of your gifts, you can hear His Voice speaking to you. He wants to walk intimately with each of us, and He has made a way to communicate with us personally.

What He speaks to us in these quiet moments will always align with His Word. We can rest in His faithfulness to always lead us into Truth.

You may or may not be a seer; it's only one of many gifts, but you are powerfully gifted by your Creator. You are unique, and your gifts fit you perfectly. They are your destiny to walk out, and we need you to be walking in them with bold courage. I need you so I can grow and continue being who I am called to be.

Regardless of what your gifts are, it's imperative for all of us to walk intimately with Abba and humbly before Him. We must be submitted to His will above our own. We set our heart on obeying Him in all things and walking clothed in His armor, guarding what has been entrusted.

These gifts are a trust between our Father and us.

CHAPTER 38:

DOMINOES

Over the months, I settled into the love Abba held for me. It was the richest treasure in my life. I was aware of the great lengths He had gone to for my redemption, and He was teaching me how to live in His Kingdom. I spent countless hours alone with Him, being in His presence and asking hundreds, if not thousands, of questions. This was a sweet, precious time in my life. I felt safe and secure in His arms.

Not so much with people.

Other than Pastor Wayne and Deanna, my experience with people had not held many positive interactions. I didn't know what healthy friendships or relationships with people looked like. Trust towards people didn't come easily for me, and the whole concept of loving people was riddled with conflicting messages.

Learning to love others was difficult and messy. I hurt others on this part of my journey and was hurt as well. It wasn't pretty, but it's so important to share.

In my youthful exuberance, I wanted to share the freedom I had found with any and all who would listen, and even those who didn't want to know. I couldn't grasp why anyone wouldn't want to be free. I wanted everyone to experience the love I had found in Abba's arms.

In these encounters with others, I wasn't listening to Holy Spirit and certainly not being led by Him. I knew Abba wanted freedom for His people, so it never occurred to me to ask Him what to share, and even more importantly, what not to.

So, I was a loose cannon. What I saw, I said. Bluntly and with great fervor.

My intent was not to hurt or bring harm; it was to tell people they didn't need to be in bondage one more minute! It puzzled me when people were hurt or didn't want to know how they could be free.

My harsh and insensitive words were spoken out of my own immaturity. Regardless of the love I felt for the person, my actions were outside of Abba's timing. The words were not His; they were mine. Because of this, they did not carry Kingdom power to set anyone free. They were just hurtful to already wounded hearts.

I didn't understand what was happening, but I could clearly see the results. I found it incredibly sad and was struggling with what was wrong. When I came to Abba and asked Him what was going on, He said quite plainly, "I could do something here if you would get out of the way!" That set me back on my seat.

As I was still before Him, waiting for Him to explain, I saw this amazing symphony. It was playing the most beautiful music. As I listened, my spirit soared into the heavens.

The conductor was masterfully leading, coaxing from each instrument its best music possible. Together, each part fit, flowed and moved into this glorious living music.

Then my ears became attentive to this sound coming from somewhere within the orchestra. It was offbeat, out of tune and didn't blend with the rest of the symphony. It was disruptive and distracting. I wanted to shout at it to stop because it was ruining the sounds that were so beautiful.

As I began to search the source of this sound out, I realized the annoying instrument was me. In the midst of this beautiful symphony, I was off into my own world, playing my own sound. It didn't flow with the rest of the symphony; it was out of sync. It had the potential to be beautiful, but needed to be brought under the Conductor's touch. Only He could make it fit into the rest of the symphony.

It was becoming easier for me to walk in step with Abba in my personal time with Him. I hadn't learned that my relationship with others was equally dependent upon me being in tune with Him and His purposes.

My eyes were being opened to see true love flows from Him, always. Not just in the words I speak, but in His timing.

He, alone, knows where each of us is in our journey. From His knowledge as the Conductor of our lives, He is the One who directs us in our relationships with others.

He knows the time to step in, the time to be quiet, the time to offer help, and the time to simply pray. I hadn't been asking Him about any of this. I had charged on ahead of Him.

This resulted in me being controlling in my friendships, mostly to protect myself. With the little bit of Truth I had learned, I was opinionated and proud. I was impatient with people who were clinging to their wounds as their identity.

I gave money and gifts when Abba wanted to teach people dependence upon Him. I intervened in life circumstances, enabling people in unhealthy ways, rather than drawing them into a relationship with Him. I was running rampant, doing my own thing. I was that bothersome instrument playing out of tune. This caused me to alienate people I loved, destroying friendships I highly valued.

It made me sick to my stomach to know my words and actions had been used to hurt the very wounded I wanted to see set free. I was filled with grief and sorrow.

I fell on my face and repented to Abba, asking Him to forgive me and remove these ugly things from my life. I asked Him to teach me how to walk in His love towards others. I wanted every area of my life to bring Him glory, and this needed His touch in me.

I had many opportunities to grow in this over time. One of the first lessons I learned came from one of my daughters.

The habit of talking to Abba about my children was deeply ingrained in me. It started out of desperation when I was a new momma. Those early years were difficult and demanding but so very sweet.

Somehow, in my blissful ignorance, I thought as my children grew older, the need to be on my face asking for my Daddy's help would lessen. I was wrong.

The decisions my children faced as they grew up were greater and carried more weight on their future than in the formative toddler years of their lives. In my mother's heart, I wanted to jump in, to spare them any and all pain.

On this day, I was concerned about one of my daughters and the choices she was making. I knew if they continued in their current direction, it was going to bring her much hurt. I was sure I knew exactly what was wrong and knew what needed to be done.

However, in light of my recent correction from Abba, I stopped to ask Him about this. I wanted to know what He saw and what He wanted me to do. I needed to hear Him before I stepped in, but I was confident I was right in my evaluation of the situation.

As I came before Him, seeking His face on the matter, He took me into a large room. The floor was covered with rows and rows of dominoes standing on end, like I used to make as a kid. As I walked around the dominoes, I could see there was writing on them.

As I looked closer, the writing named concerns and struggles in my daughter's life. I continued moving around the room, looking intently until I found the domino I had been looking for. There it was! The very thing I had identified as my main concern for her.

Looking at it now, I saw it was connected to other things I had seen in her life. This felt like a confirmation to me, bolstering my confidence this was the domino that needed to fall. If this one fell, it would cause everything else to fall in line.

I eagerly reached out my hand to push it over when I heard my Abba speak, *"Not that one!"* Startled, I hesitated, pulling my hand back. I looked at Him, waiting for Him to help me understand.

He gently took me, and we were now hovering over the dominoes, looking down. From this place, I saw things very differently. Between the long lines of connecting dominoes, there were several short lines. These short little lines didn't intersect with the others; they were false runs. They were lures, traps, and diversions. They were like rabbit trails, going nowhere.

The domino I was about to push over, was standing at the beginning of one of those short meaningless dead ends. It would have accomplished a short burst of activity but led nowhere.

Lovingly, Abba spoke into my spirit. "From your limited view, you think you know the problem and move quickly to resolve it. When you reach out to knock this down in your own knowledge, this is deadly. Instead of freedom, this brings more wounding." As I looked back at the dominoes, I saw how True this was.

I looked at Abba and asked Him to teach me His ways. He said, "Be quick to listen for My Voice and slow to act. Take the necessary time to see through My eyes, hear with My ears, and follow hard after obeying Me. I will show you the root that needs to fall to bring about lasting changes."

We turned back to the dominoes, and He pointed to a domino that didn't look like it led anywhere. It was cleverly disguised and hidden. When I looked closer, what was written on this domino was not something I had considered as being a problem in my daughter's life.

But now that I read it written here, it made so much sense. I had been blinded to it until now because I was so sure of my own thoughts.

Abba reached out His hand and knocked the domino down. I watched in fascination as line upon line began to fall. They fell in such a way that even the ones that did not intersect were affected and fell from the thundering vibration of the momentum.

As I stood watching this unfold, I realized the domino I had thought was the issue, was one of the last to fall. What had seemed so big and glaring in my eyes wasn't what was concerning Abba.

When the shaking stopped, every barrier had been removed. Then, I watched as new dominoes were set up in an entirely new order. Written on these dominoes were amazing gifts, talents, and opportunities. With great love and care, Abba was revealing His heart towards my daughter. It changed how I viewed her as well.

This scene has played out many times in my life with various people. It broke off of me some of the rough edges. No longer was I quick to judge hearts from what I see on the surface. I am constantly trying to quiet my heart and ask Abba what He sees.

When I take the time to listen and see people through Abba's eyes, it's always a very different view from what I formed in my own mind. Gentle compassion comes when Truth is revealed, and my words and actions align with His purposes. Sweet music flows when I am yielded to the Great Conductor of all things.

As I set my heart to listen and obey His leading, the results have always been good. Not because of me, but because His heart is always towards His people. He loves them far more than I ever could. His ways are so much higher than ours, His thoughts so much greater. He is the source of all True love.

CHAPTER 39:

THE TRAIN

Seeing Abba as the source of all True love was important for me to understand. As I said before, the messages I heard about love were mixed and conflicted. I had to see love through Abba's eyes, not the standards of man.

In Abba's Kingdom, love is sacred. It is not glib or flippant. It is pure and holy.

As I continued to study, I began to see True love is founded in Truth. This was critical because Abba's Truth is non-negotiable and never changes. His Truth stands and will stand for all eternity. Truth is the foundation for True love.

This came alive for me because we are clearly told Jesus is the Truth. Truth isn't a principle, a theology, or a rule. Truth is the alive and living God, our Savior Jesus Christ.

I had lost sight of this. Now, Abba was reminding me that to know Truth is to know Him. Seeking Truth is walking with Him intimately.

As we spend time with Him, the Truth, we gain wisdom. His Truth always conforms us more and more into His image. When we are matured by wisdom, love flows through us as an overflow that can't be held back. It's a spring gushing up from deep places we find only in Him, and it's a delight to let it flow freely.

This was a beautiful picture of Abba's sacred love.

I was beginning to see that not all the things done in the name of love come from Him. There are two sources of what we often call love. One comes from the Throne of the Living God, and the other comes from the depths of Hades.

I knew firsthand what love without Truth or wisdom would do. It brought hurt, bondage, and death.

There are many things in our current culture done in the name of love that are not born out of the Truth and wisdom of Abba. Men, women, and children are abused by those who say they love them. Marriages are torn apart by empty words that do not carry Abba's love. Friendships dissolve as love remains undefined; without boundaries.

Since the enemy can't create, he counterfeits. Love is no different.

The enemy is creating mixed messages with the intent to thwart True love from reigning in our lives. In our ignorance, we don't expect to find his evil devices here. Not when everything is being done in the name of love.

I had to wake up and see that when love is no longer sacred, no longer flowing from Abba, it becomes a license for all kinds of evil. When people accept the lie that as long as you can say something is done in love and everything is permissible, our society breaks down and the enemy laughs.

This fleshly reasoning protects all types of evil by declaring carnal words or actions as untouchable. They are not open for discussion or available to be tested and tried through the Word of God. This kind of love the enemy feeds us rejects all discernment and opposes correction.

Again, for me to understand True love, I had to see it was founded only upon the Word of God. Anything less is the sad state of affairs mentioned in scriptures where every man is doing what is right in his own eyes.

We are clearly warned there is a way that seems right to our own natural understanding, but the end is our destruction if it isn't tested through Abba's Word.

As Abba was speaking this to me, I found myself in a vision by a train track. This was in the middle of nowhere. There wasn't a train depot; just a wooden platform that I was standing on.

I began walking along the tracks because I could see a train trestle ahead. The tracks brought me to the edge of a deep narrow gorge with a raging river several hundred feet below. It was breathtakingly beautiful.

As I tried to follow the tracks to the other side, I realized they ended in the middle of the trestle. The end of the line was to plummet into the depths of the ravine to certain death.

At that moment, I heard a train whistle behind me. My heart dropped, and I ran as quickly as I could back to the platform, hoping the train would stop. When I got back to the platform, I began waving my arms and screaming for the train to stop.

It barreled by me, not even slowing down. I could see into the train cars. The people were laughing, partying, doing all kinds of everyday things with absolutely no understanding of what was coming quickly. Every once in a while, I made eye contact with someone on the train, and I was sobbing for them to get off the train because it was clear it wasn't going to stop.

Every so often, the doors would fly open, and someone would jump off the train, tumble down the rocky embankment and get up dazed. As I was jumping up and down screaming until I had no voice, they looked ahead and realized the tracks ended. They, too, began screaming for their friends and families to get off the train and once in a while, the doors would open, and someone would jump.

I found myself sobbing and asking Abba to please open the eyes of His people to the lies and schemes of the enemy. The powers of darkness are steering this train we call life into a dark end if we do not come into an intimate relationship with Abba through His Son, Jesus Christ.

I've seen the evil fruit of false love. I've spoken with many young people who bought into the lie of this false love that allowed them to do whatever they pleased with no consequences. Only, life doesn't work that way. They found that out as they were shipwrecked on the shores of despair and disillusionment - many at the point of suicide.

The answer for them is the same as the answer was for me and for each of us: coming to a place of repentance for believing that love can flow from any place other than the heart of Jesus, our Savior and Lord.

There is no love apart from Abba. True love is found only through the cross of Jesus Christ.

The enemy wants to keep us in bondage and will use every scheme he can to accomplish his plan of destruction in our lives. False love is one of his best schemes because it promises everything and delivers nothing.

Remember, the enemy doesn't actually want us; he simply wants to keep us from Abba. The enemy's goal is to separate us from the presence of Abba eternally.

If we lose Abba's presence, we lose all that is good, right, holy, pure, peaceable, and joyful. Without His presence, there is no love. This, I've come to believe, is the greatest hell there is.

CHAPTER 40:

PEAKS AND VALLEYS

Abba lovingly gave me six precious years of being mentored by Pastor Wayne and Deanna. Finally, they were called to a different state to minister. Although we lost touch for a few years, they never ceased to pray for me. Today, we are still in contact, and I am daily grateful for their love shown to me. They will always hold a special place in my heart.

Many seasons of my life have passed since Abba so graciously and mercifully imparted these powerful Truths into the core of my being. It took several years for me to see the depths of the treasures of Truth I had been given.

These lessons were wonderful mountain top times in my life. I received sweet promises from Abba. As I looked across to the next mountain where the fulfillment of those promises was being held, my heart was filled with courage and great joy.

However, maturity doesn't come from the head knowledge gained on the mountain tops. It comes when I start heading down into the valley to walk out the Truth I had been given.

My experience has been that those valleys can be rough.

They hold hidden traps and snares that, quite honestly, I didn't know if I would make it through. There were many times I just wasn't sure I could. Sometimes, curling up in a fetal position with my head under a pillow seemed like the best option.

I walked through the failure of my 24-year marriage. I watched as some of my children walked away from God, trying to find love in the ways of the world, filling empty voids with all manner of things resulting in great harm.

I've known loneliness, betrayal, rejection, and accusation beyond what I thought my heart could take. I realized that some people liked me broken and wounded. When I was in that place, I was easily manipulated and controlled.

But Abba doesn't want us to stay in a place of brokenness; He wants us whole! He doesn't want us to live as victims, but as overcomers through the power of the shed blood of His Son, Jesus. Sometimes, relationships based on wounding and abuse will end as we heal.

This was one of the hardest lessons about True love I ever had to learn.

Over many years of warring in the heavenlies and seeing many wonderful victories over people's lives, I was sidetracked. I had come to think if I prayed long enough, warred hard enough, fasted and stood strong, Abba would change people. My marriage would be saved.

Not only is this very wrong, but it is also extremely dangerous.

Years earlier, Pastor Wayne had issued a warning to me. He told me, "If the enemy can't hold you back, he'll shove you over."

Well, I wasn't turning back, but I did get shoved over a time or two, or eighty-six and more.

What was dangerous about where my natural reasoning had gone was it defied the very essence of humanity as Abba created us. It violated free will.

Each of us was created with free will by Abba's design. He didn't want us to be robots who simply followed Him because we had no other options. No, He wants us to follow Him because we choose to.

So, as I watched my marriage fail and later had my children walk away, Abba so sweetly came and reminded me, "My love gives people the power to choose, even when their choices rip your heart out."

As I sat on the floor in a crumpled heap crying puddles of tears, I saw clearly what His love had suffered for me. Had I not betrayed Him with my actions so many times? Had I not rejected His Truth and tried my own way?

Yet He loved me still. He loved me while I was unlovable. I am able to love others because I am secure in His love, even when the choices they are making bring great hurt and pain to my heart.

True love demands that after we have done all we can in prayer and intercession to drive back the powers of darkness from blinding eyes and whispering lies, we give others the freedom to make their choice. They must choose which kingdom they will live in and which Master they will serve.

Each one of us is free to make this choice. There are also consequences in the choices we make, whether good or evil. Likewise, the choices made in these junctures oftentimes affect our relationships. Rebellion against Abba always brings division.

One thing I've learned: Abba is a faithful Father. His love for them will never cease. He will pursue them and go to great lengths to bring each one into eternity with Him. He loves them far more than I ever could, and He knows the plans He has for each one. There is no safer place for them to be than put gently and lovingly upon His altar for Him to do what He alone can. I know the character of My Abba; He is trustworthy with those most precious to me.

It is the most difficult expression of True love to release those we love to their choices and entrust them into Abba's care. Then, in trusting faith that He has them, continue on our journey of intimacy with Him.

I share this because I've sat in too many conferences, churches, and small groups where the speakers seemed to have it all together. Everything in their life was perfect, their children were all following God, and they had need of nothing.

As much as I rejoice with them, this has not been my story. I can't relate to those kinds of testimonies because my life has been messy.

Most of this, I brought on myself as I struggled to grow up or through making some really bad decisions. Some of it was inflicted by others, to which I had to find my way to forgive and heal. Regardless, my life has not been neat and tidy.

Yet it was in the midst of the messiness that I found Abba to be more than loving, kind, gracious, and faithful. It was in the darkest seasons of my life when He came alongside me, picked me up out of the mud, brushed me off, and drew me into His arms with His true love and acceptance.

It was in those valleys where I learned the power of His Word as the Sword of the Spirit. When the enemy tried to come in like a flood to utterly sweep me away, I found courage behind His Shield of Faith.

One important lesson time has taught me is this; when we follow after Abba's Kingdom with all of our heart, soul, mind, and strength, it doesn't mean everything in our lives is going to be all roses.

What it does mean is we never walk alone. It means He comes in power when we cry out to Him. He bought us with a high price, gave His only Son to redeem us, filled us with His Spirit to establish us in His Truth, all so we could be restored to walk intimately with Him. His power to keep us is greater than the enemy's power to destroy us.

Abba has a path for His people. It is outlined in His Word and has concise boundaries. These boundaries are not to limit our fun or minimize our life as the enemy works hard to convince us. No, they are boundaries created by His True love.

Walking in His Truth offers security and peace when we stay within His precepts and principles. We can run, jump, play, sing, and dance freely in His grace and favor. When storms come, He is right beside us as a strong tower, a refuge, and a secure place to run to.

CHAPTER 41:

NEW GARDEN

As I was spending time with Abba on this particular day, I saw in my spirit that we were walking in a field towards a beautiful garden. It had a white picket fence around it with an arched entrance. Gardening is something I enjoy, so this was special to me.

As we drew near, I could see this garden had been lovingly tended. The soil was rich, brown, and soft. I took my shoes off at the gate to walk in the warm soil. The rows were well kept, and this garden had been well weeded.

Between the fruitful plants were beautiful flowers. Flowers also lined the fence both inside and out. The bees and butterflies were enjoying the nectar. It was a welcoming and refreshing place to be.

As I sat on the bench inside this garden with a gentle breeze blowing the sweet scent of the soil to me, Abba said, "This garden is your heart. You have worked hard to make it a place for us to walk intimately together. It is bringing forth a good yield, and many are drawn here. You have done well."

Then, He looked over to a piece of land that was barren; the soil had never been worked. He said, "I want you to take what you have learned here and begin a new work there." He pointed to a place filled with rocks and old stumps. I was unable to see if the soil would even be good to grow anything. Yet somehow, this place called to me.

I opened the gate, walked over to this barren place, and absent-mindedly began picking up rocks to make a border. As I worked, excitement grew in my heart to see this ground flourish. Even though I knew it was going to be a lot of work, I felt hopeful at what this could become.

As I came across the stumps, I wondered what tragedy had taken the trees down, leaving these old stumps with deep roots in the midst of this place. I started thinking about my own life and wondered if there were still stumps of wounding in me I hadn't seen yet.

Abba stood beside me, listening to the questions of my heart. He gently said, "I will bring healing when you have the courage to face the source of the pain."

In that moment, I knew it was true. I could look back on the years and see Abba's hand. He would plant new Truths into my heart, and when they had grown deep, and I was secure in them, He would reveal areas of wounding in my life needing His healing touch. I believe this is a lifelong process, guided by His hand.

Resting in His great love for me, I knew I didn't have to hunt through my heart for all the stumps. He would reveal them in His perfect time, and we would face healing like we faced everything: together.

I set my face back to the task at hand; my heart was at rest. I found myself wondering with child-like excitement what this new garden would yield. It wouldn't take long for Abba to reveal His plans.

CHAPTER 42:

ACCEPTED IN THE BELOVED

It was one of those beautiful Texas evenings with the sun starting to hang low in the sky. After several years, I had recently remarried, and was enjoying this new season of my life. My husband, Michael, suggested a country drive. It's a favorite thing we do.

As we traveled along, we were talking with each other and Abba about the wonder of all the ways He expresses His love towards us. As we drove, my hand was held lovingly in Michael's, as is his way. My heart was once again filled with thanksgiving for this man beside me. For the first time in my life, I knew what it meant to be cherished.

We had driven for about an hour, enjoying the journey with worship music playing softly. I had no idea where we were headed; I just enjoyed being with this precious man Abba had brought into my life.

We were long past anything of the city when we came upon an oak-filled pasture. Without a word, my husband pulled the truck over. He came around and opened my door, and we both walked up to the fence alongside the road.

There, in the sunset light was a herd of cattle. Alongside the mommas were several new spring calves. A cry of joy came from deep within me as I tried not to startle them. I turned to my husband. How deeply this man knows me and loves me well. He knew I wouldn't only want to see them, but I needed to hear them as well.

There I stood with Michael's arm around me, letting my heart be fed by the sound of a new momma welcoming her precious baby. I waited until I heard it. There it was, coming to us on the warm Texas breeze, the most precious sound in the world to me. A momma cow lowing to her newborn, a sound reserved just for this moment.

There is not a sweeter sound to my ears.

I couldn't help looking back on the day when a very little girl sat high up on the hay in her folk's barn, longing to know True love. I remember the scene as if it were yesterday. I always will.

The scene doesn't bring my heart pain anymore. Instead, a joyful smile comes to my face and a song fills my heart, as grateful tears start to roll down my face. My husband hugged me just a bit tighter because He knows.

You see, I found the love my child's heart sought so many years ago in the arms of my Heavenly Father, my Abba.

Just like that newborn calf from years before answered to his momma's lowing, I had come to know the gentle Voice of my Daddy. It is the Voice He uses only between Him and me when He speaks to my heart.

It welcomed me into a fierce world I had been abruptly dropped into. It brings comfort to my frightened heart when I face things that are bigger than me. It protects, defends, and loves me with an everlasting love that will never pass away.

He has declared my value and worth in His sight! I am His.

My Abba Daddy has made me accepted as His beloved. My home is in Him.

Welcome home, little one!

EPILOGUE

This is a story of hope in the middle of real-life horrible tragedies we endure. There is so much hurt in the world today.

The more time I spend with people, the more I know each of us carries our own pain. The world is just cruel sometimes. One source of pain is no greater or no less than another. It is not to be compared, weighed, or measured. Pain is pain.

Hurt wounds us deeply, leaving its ugly mark. It can cause us to feel like a damaged canoe set adrift in the vast ocean with no paddle. Alone. Damaged. Drifting. Hopeless. Useless. Pain makes us doubt we'll ever touch dry land again.

Abba desires to set us free from the rejection, betrayal, and abandonment we have endured. He hates the verbal, physical, sexual, financial, and emotional abuse we have suffered.

He has seen us being manipulated and our identity being cruelly crushed. He detests the molestations, sexual abuses, and humiliations we bore to fulfill the lusts of evil people.

The pain we suffer has the ability to change us in good or bad ways. The beauty of it is, we get to choose what to do with our pain!

Each one of us can find new life, new hope, and new purpose to go on living fully and freely. The wounds we suffered can be healed; we can overcome the pain, and we can live in peace with purpose and joy. Truly, the precious blood of our Lord and Savior, Jesus Christ, overcomes everything we have suffered.

He is very near to the brokenhearted; His ears are always open to their cry. He came to set the captives free, to bind up our wounds, and to give us His life.

What the enemy meant for our harm and destruction, when submitted and yielded at the foot of the cross, becomes a weapon of war in our hand to reveal and destroy the works of darkness in us. As overcomers, we are given Abba's power to share His freedom with others.

My earnest prayer for each one of you is that Jesus meets you right where you are and holds you close. May His peace wash over your weary heart. May you know the great love that He has for you.

My prayer is that in the depths of your heart, God's word will set you free to enter into His Truth. You are the apple of His eye. He wants to walk intimately with you.

Your wounds matter to Him!

"Blessed be the God and Father of our Lord Jesus Christ, who hath blessed us with all spiritual blessings in heavenly places.

According as He hath *chosen us* before the foundations of the world, that we should be holy and without blame before Him in love!

Having called us unto the adoption of children by Jesus Christ to Himself; according to the good pleasure of His will.

To the praise of the glory of His grace, Wherein

HE HATH MADE US ACCEPTED IN THE BELOVED!!!!!!!!"

Ephesians 1:3-6

JESUS

We are born into this battle because of the fall of man in the garden. It's not something we chose; it's bequeathed at birth. This compelling urge to sin is wired into our earthly minds and carried out by our bodies. None of us escape its evil clutches.

Then Abba sent Jesus.

Jesus came to conquer sin, death, and the grave by being the ultimate sacrificial Lamb of God. His blood was spilled and paid the price for our redemption. His blood is our atonement. He gave His life to be our Redeemer.

Jesus' death did not spell defeat for the Kingdom of God. It was the birthing ground of something so much better. That precious blood spilled on the ground became the holy fertilizer from which new life would spring.

We must never forget that Jesus was God's Son. He was born of a woman so he could identify with our temptations and troubles as a man. He was also born of God, so the power living in Him far surpassed anything the enemy could do.

Jesus willingly chose to suffer and die for our redemption. As the enemy sought to kill Him, He knew what the enemy did not. He would not stay dead.

Death could not hold him, and the grave could not contain Him because He is born of God. When He died, He descended into the pit of hades and confronted the host of darkness who dwelt there. He went in power and authority gained by the shedding of His blood.

He had in His hand the key to unlock the prison doors that held His people. The enemy was helpless to stop him as He ransomed His people from that place, leading them into the courts of heaven. His blood paid their debt to sin, and they were set free eternally.

When we call upon the Name of Jesus to be saved, we are asking to be set free from the law of sin and death through His sacrifice, His shed blood. We are repentant of our sins that Jesus suffered and died to deliver us from. We are acknowledging that apart from His atonement, we have no hope of being restored to our Heavenly Father.

By accepting His beautiful gift of grace extended to us, we are choosing to die to our old sin nature. Our intent is not to return to our old ways of living. We are exchanging our citizenship in this world for His Kingdom. Old things pass away through the cross, we are washed clean by His blood, and all things become new. We enter a new realm in which we now live.

This is revealed and demonstrated through water baptism. We are entering into the death, burial, and resurrection of Jesus Christ as our Lord and Savior. We are raised up in a new Kingdom to live new lives in Him. His Spirit fills us with Himself, and everything has now changed. Everything!

We are now serving a new King. We are living by His laws. We have been set free from our sinful nature that ruled our flesh, and we now set our will to walk in a manner worthy of His calling. Our old nature has been crucified and is dead to us.

Through the blood of Jesus Christ, we have been adopted into the family of God. He is now our Father, and we are His children. We belong to Him.

The life we now live is lived by faith in Jesus Christ. We have been set free to walk in obedience to His ways, which are so much higher than our old ways. We walk after His purposes to fulfill His will just as Jesus walked only after His Father's will.

Jesus said nothing and did nothing apart from His Father. He spent time alone with Him to know His will, and He stayed yielded to His Father in all things, even unto death.

As believers in Jesus Christ, we are hungry to know Him and to love Him His way. We study the Word of God to learn His ways because living in the Kingdom of God is vastly different than what we've ever known before. God's economy does not run on the same principles as the earthly realm.

Through His resurrection, victory for us to stand against the wiles and schemes of the enemy was won. The same power that overcame death, conquered the stronghold of sin, vanquished the hold of the grave, and raised Jesus from the dead now lives in us who choose Him as our Lord and Savior.

From His place at the right hand of His Father, Jesus gave us His authority to go into the world in His Name. We overcome by the Blood of the Lamb, the word of our testimony and we don't love our lives even unto death.

ABOUT THE AUTHOR

Nancy Everist lives in the Texas Hill Country with her husband, Michael, and their two dogs. They are avid hikers who enjoy the beauty of Abba's creation.

She would love to hear how "Accepted" has impacted your life and pray for you as Holy Spirit leads. Nancy can be reached at:
Nancy@yourgreatestrace.com

Nancy and Michael travel and speak about their respective stories of deliverance and healing. They teach on spiritual warfare as it flows from an intimate relationship with Abba, our Heavenly Father. Their hearts are fixed on equipping the remnant to stand against the schemes and wiles of the enemy and walk as more than conquerors through Jesus Christ.

Visit their website for information and resources:
www.nancyzeverist.com

ABOUT THE GLOVERS

Since the writing of this book, Pastor Wayne and Deanna Glover have retired from full time pastoral ministry. As faithful shepherds, they further the work of the Kingdom.

They continue to walk people through deliverance and are available to speak on this very important topic. They can be reached at: Wdglover3@msn.com

Made in the USA
Monee, IL
04 March 2022